LAY PASTORAL
CARE GIVING

Timothy M. Farabaugh

DISCIPLESHIP RESOURCES

P O BOX 340003 • NASHVILLE, TN 37203-0003
www.discipleshipresources.org

LAY PASTORAL CARE GIVING

ISBN 978-0-88177-554-9
Library of Congress Control Number 2008943962

I would like to dedicate this book to my wife, Debby, who continues to support me in my ministry and my writing; and both my father and father-in-law, whose lives of faithful examples have given me inspiration and hope. I would also like to acknowledge the assistance of my son-in-law, Michael Stafford, in retrieving most of this book from a hard drive that crashed. Thank you all very much!

CONTENTS

INTRODUCTION

Lay pastoral caregiving is a term used to describe a program of providing pastoral care to the members of the congregation using laity that have gone through a training program and are assigned and supervised by the church pastor.

In this book, I will use both Scripture and history to support the need for such a program, then spell out step by step how this program can work in the local church. Finally, the book will provide the pastor with valuable information to share with the lay pastoral caregivers as they go through their initial training and the monthly support meetings required to enable the lay pastoral caregiver to gain information and support for their ministry.

While serving at Christ United Methodist Church in Bethel Park, Pennsylvania, I met Ronald H. Sunderland, Ed. D., who had developed a training program called "Equipping Laypeople for Ministry." Using what I learned from Dr. Sunderland, I trained and supervised laity in my congregation and in other churches in lay pastoral caregiving.

At a meeting of the Alexandria District Council on Ministries several years ago, our conversation focused on the realization that most of the clergy had no assistance in the area of pastoral care and felt overwhelmed by their many, sometimes conflicting, responsibilities. While a few churches used the Stephen Ministry material and others used different materials to train church members in caring ministries, most of the churches did not train *anyone* in caring ministries. The District Superintendent encouraged me to put together such a program that could help churches of all sizes. As a District Council on Ministries, we did not envision the training program compulsory for the churches; however, we did hope that the training would increase the pastoral care the members of the congregations could receive.

From past experience and much discussion, I determined a ministry of lay pastoral caregiving needed 1) clergy support; 2) congregation acceptance; and 3) ongoing training. These three components became the cornerstone of this program.

The clergy are involved in selecting laity to serve as lay pastoral caregivers. They lead them through the initial weekend training and assign these laity to visit people in need. Following the visits, the clergy review what happened in the visit and offers direction and encouragement. After the initial training, we held services of dedication to introduce further the concept of lay pastoral caregiving to the entire congregation. The clergy then provide continuing training to the caregivers at monthly meetings.

The practical reality of this training program is that more congregation members receive visits from someone who has had training in pastoral care. These visits may be a single check-in visit or regular fortnightly visits. Lay pastoral care will not take the place of the clergy also providing pastoral care. In fact, the feedback from the laity will keep the clergy well informed of the needs of the congregation. More time will be required of the clergy to train and supervise the lay pastoral caregivers, but the congregation will receive a much deeper and broader care from clergy and from gifted and trained laity.

In the Bible we learn much about the gifts within the body of Christ. Ephesians 4:11-13 offers magnificent words about the purpose of these gifts: to "equip the saints for the work of ministry, for building the body of Christ, until all should come to the unity of the faith. . . ." We consistently affirm a theological perspective that speaks of the priesthood of all believers. The laypeople of the church are at the core of every aspect of ministry. Ministries of Christian education, missions, finance, evangelism, and stewardship do not happen without whole church participation. Today it is time for clergy and laity to partner in caring for one another in the church.

—Timothy Farabaugh

PART I

Overview

Case for Lay Pastoral Care Giving

To begin to write about lay pastoral care giving means to write about myself and my beliefs about the church as the body of Christ. I am an ordained United Methodist clergyman, and my bishop appointed me to serve as the administrator of a continuing care retirement center in the Virginia suburbs outside Washington, D.C. I get to meet many different people and deal with many different matters that might seem far removed from the functions of ministry that my clergy sisters and brothers may do. You might imagine that the everyday issues in a retirement center differ from the everyday issues in the life of a church. However, my clergy sisters and brothers and I have one thing in common: We all care for other people.

From my vantage point at the Hermitage, I see people caring for others on a daily basis. I see staff and volunteers caring for the residents and for one another. While some might assume that this caring could mean the physical needs of those in our healthcare area, I am not referring to that. I mean that every day people in our facility show caring by listening to residents' and staff members' concerns for children or grandchildren or great-grandchildren. Staff members show caring by listening to problems that are not medically based. Volunteer visitors show love and caring by their presence and by their attentiveness to those they visit. For example, a nurse may give a shot, but the manner in which that nurse gives the shot and attends to the needs of the recipient will communicate whether that nurse cares or loves or feels compassionate about the individual receiving the medication. Here is another example: One church group comes to sing Christmas carols because it is the season of Advent. Other church groups visit retirement communities all the time. Can you see a difference in commitment and caring in the church group that visits once a month or visits once a year? Or the group in which the members visit with the residents before or after a performance?

By our presence and by our attitudes, we communicate our own experience of the love and compassion of God in Jesus Christ. By such a presence with others, we witness to our knowledge of God's love. This is what Christians do: We witness to the redeeming love of Jesus Christ.

Lay pastoral care giving is the best team or even community approach to the care of souls within a congregation. One of the traditional understandings of pastoral responsibility has been that the pastor was the primary person responsible for the care of souls. Throughout church history, the role of pastor meant the leading of worship and the visitation of the sick and dying. Pastors visited those in need and generally went from home to home to minister to those within the pastoral flock. In other times, clergy lived with different time demands. For example, they did not face long commutes to hospitals or traffic jams. They did not have multilevel administrative meetings nor did they have to deal with local government zoning boards. Contemporary clergy need training in Safe Sanctuaries® practices and a variety of continuing education courses not imagined fifty years ago. They need skills in planning and leadership and team building, fund development and community organization and sometimes, even plumbing skills. In many ways today, clergy are the least focused on the care of souls because of the many other demands placed upon them.

Church history gives us examples of heroic pastors who held on no matter what happened and cared for the souls entrusted to them. One example of such a pastor is Martin Rinkart, who ministered in the seventeenth century during the Thirty Years' War and a time of plague. Because of the many deaths from plague and starvation, Rinkart conducted as many as fifty funerals a day and buried thousands from his city. Despite this workload, Rinkart wrote the hymn we know as "Now Thank We All Our God," and the hymn witnesses to the enduring faith of a pastor who dealt with harsh conditions and cared for souls.

I am not saying that clergy today do not care for souls. I hope no one walks away from this book with that notion. I am saying that today clergy and laity can work together in new and creative ways to care for souls. This is the team-based approach to pastoral care that we need. We see people in daily ministry who care for souls. They are doctors, nurses, counselors, and teachers. They are parents, neighbors, friends, and older adults. They are the school crossing guards, firefighters, and workers at the YMCA and YWCA. Now is the time to become much more intentional about such care giving.

Lay pastoral care giving is based on the idea that the church wastes the gifts of community when it does not encourage and empower the laity to use their gifts. The model I offer includes training in specific skills and life concerns. It includes a time of reporting back to a pastor or other ordained person—not in a hierarchical model, but because the care of souls is a primary responsibility of pastors, I believe that this model of lay pastoral care giving offers a healthy, community-based approach that empowers many people for new and creative forms of ministry. In most denominations, the laity serves in a variety of ways within the institution of the church and beyond it in a variety of ministries. Here we seek to identify the spiritual gifts of those in the congregation who will serve as lay pastoral caregivers. As a church, we will provide training, encouragement, and opportunity to enable these caregivers to succeed in new forms of ministry.

Lay people serve their churches in a variety of ways. They lead and serve on committees to understand vision and mission. They carry out work in areas such as worship, evangelism, mission, stewardship, and Christian education, but congregations have, for the most part, ignored the area of pastoral care. The church has generally assumed that such a role belongs solely to the clergy. One of the most valid reasons for this is the nature of confidentiality that must be part of every pastoral care or counseling experience, and this is an aspect of lay care giving that will be addressed. I will say again that the pastoral work has become too complex and that the laity of the church are indeed willing and able to take on this ministry of caring.

A word of caution concerning limits and boundaries: This program does not intend to train laity to be pastoral counselors. I invite clergy and laity to use their gifts together to become good listeners and pastoral care-givers. In doing so, the church will begin to recognize the gifts and graces often hidden within every congregation.

Biblical and Theological Premise

Several Scripture passages help explain the nature of laity involved in pastoral caregiving. They refer to spiritual gifts and the guidance of the Holy Spirit for every Christian to do God's will in his or her life and to help establish God's kingdom on Earth.

Begin with Ephesians 4:11-12: "And his gifts were that some should be apostles, some prophets, some evangelists, some pastors and teachers, to equip the saints for the work of ministry, for building up the body of Christ." Consider the importance of the word *equip*. Every person in the body of Christ contributes to the larger work of ministry quite simply because God equips each of us for such work. Lay pastoral caregivers have gifts to assist the clergy in their pastoral duties. Through this program, clergy will learn to recognize the gifts of the laity and learn how to encourage them to use their gifts for the good of the congregation.

A simple way to determine if a parishioner has a pastoral gift is to look for the people in the congregation that others turn to when they need to talk, to share a concern, or to tell their troubles. The person who is the best caregiver is a good listener. To a large extent, pastoral care is simply being present, being available, and being open to hear the needs and concerns of others.

In John 1:14 we read "the Word became flesh and dwelt among us." God dwells with us with the grace and the truth that only God can provide. For John, Jesus represents one who "is and will be present," and humankind finds its wholeness in Christ. Think also of John 10:10: "I came that they may have life, and have it abundantly." Such abundant life refers to wholeness and shalom on earth, as well as in heaven.

After the resurrection, Jesus breathed on his disciples and said, "As the Father has sent me, even so I send you." (John 20:19-23) Jesus then said, "Receive the Holy Spirit," and blessed the disciples. That same Spirit abides with disciples today—whether ordained or laity—and enables all to work on God's behalf. In the midst of providing care, clergy and lay pastoral caregivers alike lean on the support and direction of the Holy Spirit. As Christians we believe that the spirit gives us certain gifts. By using these gifts, we continue the ministry begun by Jesus.

In Matthew 1:23 Jesus is called Emmanuel, "God with us." At the end of that same gospel (Matthew 28:18-20), the disciples receive a command from Jesus to go and make disciples. Jesus promises that he will be with the disciples until the end of the age. That promise emboldens everyone to take on new ministries and to follow the leading of the Spirit.

I am an ordained United Methodist pastor. The theological insights of John Wesley shape my understanding. Whether or not you are a Wesleyan, I hope that my theological exploration will be in accord with your beliefs about God, Jesus Christ, the Holy Spirit, and the purpose of the church. Wesleyans describe the presence of the Spirit running ahead of the believer as prevenient, or preparing, grace. The Spirit heaps upon us gifts and strengths that enable us to minister to one another. With the help of the Spirit, prayers are heard, hearts uplifted, and all are shown the way. God works in the lives of Christians so that they can work for others. One of the important teachings of the Wesleyan tradition is that inward and spiritual growth is validated through outward and visible expressions of faith. Those who are fed by the sacraments and worship are able to step out to care for others, to be compassionate, to serve as an expression of a faithful follower to those who need an example, or a helping hand. Through worship and other acts of piety, such as daily Bible reading and prayer and fasting, the soul is replenished and we are enabled to continue to minister to others. Simply put, we can only give so much of ourselves spiritually and emotionally before we are recharged through receiving from God and from others. Bible study, prayer, regular devotional times, spiritual retreats, group sharing of common concerns all help recharge the lay caregiver and the pastor alike.

Lay pastoral care giving is, like many ideas, new and also based on insights gained from others. Many people, for example, engage in Stephen Ministry, a program developed by the Rev. Dr. Kenneth Haugk. I appreciate very much what Dr. Haugk did to train such caregivers, and I appreciate the work of those who are Stephen Ministers. I have learned from Dr. Haugk and from scholars as different as Howard Clinebell, Howard Stone, and Daniel Day Williams. All of these have written about caring ministries. I know that some other models of lay caring exist that offer very limited training of volunteers, and that these programs lack any follow-through training or contact. Based on my experience with churches in Virginia, I believe that churches that engage in my model of lay pastoral care giving will find a more holistic approach to ministry. You will find the team meeting and continuous learning approach offers room for growth in caring skills and knowledge. Congregations will find that their ministries within the community of faith and the broader community will grow in quality and in quantity.

Lay pastoral care giving is right for this time. As we face scheduling needs in the midst of 24/7 thinking, the team approach to ministry in a caring and compassionate way under the guidance of a pastor affirms Scripture and keeps us aware of the importance of the ministry of all believers. God bless you as you begin this journey of care!

Additional Resources

Christian Caregiving a Way of Life, by Kenneth C. Haugk

The Laity in Ministry the Whole People of God for the Whole World, by George Peck and John S. Hoffman

Lay Shepherding a Guide for Visiting the Sick, the Aged, the Troubled and the Bereaved, by Rudolph E. Grantham

Lay Ministry: A Theological, Spiritual and Pastoral Handbook, by William J. Rademacher

Ministry of the Saints: Rediscovering the Destiny of Every Believer, by Mark Hanby

Partners in Ministry: Laity and Pastors Working Together, by James L. Garlow

Chapter One Review

1. Read Ephesians 4:11-12. What word or phrase seems to attract your attention? What do these verses tell you about the church?

2. After reading Matthew 28:16-20, think about the response of the disciples. How might they have felt concerning these instructions? How do these words shape your understanding of ministry and mission?

3. Read John 10: 1-10. What insights about discipleship do you gain from these verses? How do these verses relate to lay caregiving?

CHAPTER TWO

Program Outline

Lay Pastoral Caregiving has four major purposes:

1. To assist the clergy in providing the necessary pastoral support to the congregation.
2. To select laity to serve as lay pastoral caregivers.
3. To equip these laity for this unique ministry.
4. To support and encourage the lay pastoral caregivers as they minister to fellow laity in a variety of ways.

Establishing the Lay Pastoral Caregiver Program

Explain to the governing board or, if more appropriate, a smaller group that reports to the board, the concepts proposed by this book. Here is a basic summary:

Selected laity will be invited to go through a training program that will give them skills in certain areas of pastoral care, particularly listening. The lay pastoral caregivers will meet monthly and receive additional training each month. The pastor will give monthly assignments to the lay pastoral caregivers to visit members of the congregation. These may be people who are ill, shut-in, estranged from the congregation, new parents, those who are grieving or going through a difficult time. Once the lay pastoral caregiver visits with the person to whom they have been assigned, the lay caregiver will report back to the minister and discuss appropriate next steps.

Selecting the Caregivers

The pastor and other church leaders will use their gifts of discernment to select the laity to be trained. One way to engage in such discernment is to read aloud Ephesians 4:11-12 and invite the leadership group to reflect in silence on the meaning of these verses within the context of the particular congregation. After an appropriate period of silence (3-5 minutes), ask the group to take turns and to name something they heard that connected to caring within the congregation. Then read aloud John 10:1-10 and ask the group to think about individuals in the church who exhibit compassion and caring skills. After another 3-5 minute period of silence, ask the group to name those individuals. List these names on a chalkboard or on newsprint. These are the people to whom members of the congregation have turned in the past to share their problems.

The pastor will extend an invitation to become a lay pastoral caregiver. Extend this invitation in person rather than by letter so that the pastor can explain what the program entails and why the person has been selected. You may wish to invite the potential lay caregivers to an informational meeting so that the program explanation is done only once for everyone.

Those laity who decide to commit to the training for this program must be prepared to spend one weekend in the introductory training that is led by the pastor and also to meet for additional hour-long training times as part of a regular monthly meeting where assignments are discussed and encouragement given by the lay pastoral caregiving team. In addition, they will take on assignments as directed by the pastor, make the necessary visits as agreed upon with the pastor and the person to whom they are assigned, and to report on the visit in writing. In some cases, a brief one-on-one discussion with the pastor may be necessary for guidance or additional support. The expectation is that the lay pastoral caregiver will serve in this capacity for a minimum of one year.

Training the Caregivers

Those who accept the offer to go through the training will make up the class. It is best to keep the class small enough to allow a good deal of conversation during the training. An ideal group may be between eight and fifteen persons. The training should begin with a review of the Scripture from the previous chapter and continue with the topics outlined in parts I and II of this book. (The subjects in Part III of this book will be studied in depth in the monthly training sessions.) The major emphasis in this initial training will be on understanding people's needs and on communication skills. There will also be some practical training around how the program works and how reporting is done. This training may be done in a retreat setting to allow time for team building and bonding as well as education. A Friday night and all day Saturday works best. If this is not possible, four evenings with two hours allotted each night for training may work.

An example of a possible weekend training program outline could be as follows:

Friday evening: supper, getting acquainted and introduction of program
- 6:00-7:00 Introductions and supper
- 7:00-8:30 Bible study and go over the material in Part I
- 8:30-9:00 Worship and sharing of prayer concerns

Saturday
- 7:30-8:30 Breakfast
- 8:30-9:00 Gathering
- 9:00-10:30 Brief overview of Part II and chapter 3 "Making, Keeping, & Reporting the Appointment"
- 10:30-10:45 Break
- 10:45-12:00 Chapter 4, "Pastoral Tools"
- 12:00-1:00 Lunch

- 1:00-2:30 Chapter 5 "Developmental Understandings Relevant to Pastoral Care," Ego Development and Passages
- 2:30-2:45 Break
- 2:45-4:15 Chapter 5 "Developmental Understandings Relevant to Pastoral Care," Faith Development and Christian Nurture in Normal Stages of Human Development
- 4:15-4:30 Break
- 4:30-4:45 Review of Parts I and II
- 4:45 Closing worship

As soon as possible after the initial training weekend, the pastor should ask each of the lay pastoral caregivers in turn to accompany him or her on a pastoral visit to someone they would like them to visit on their own as a follow-up. An example might be that someone is just recovering from hip surgery. One of the lay pastoral caregivers my have just had a similar experience or perhaps their parents had a similar experience. Trying to connect the right lay pastoral caregiver to the parishioner is an important part of the success of this program.

After the visit, the pastor and the lay pastoral caregiver should spend some time reviewing what they heard, saw, felt, and sensed about the visit. This review time becomes another teaching session. The pastor should explain how to listen intently so that the lay pastoral caregiver can write a verbatim of the visit. (See "Writing a Verbatim" in chapter 3.)

In addition to the verbatim, the lay pastoral caregiver then should write a short report to recommend a follow-up plan for the person visited. In some cases, no additional visits will be necessary. In other cases, many more visits will be required. When the pastor receives the report, he or she should respond in writing or by another means the appropriate response for the lay pastoral caregiver.

It may be appropriate to use a form for this reporting and to make assignments so that records may be kept, but they are not absolutely necessary so long as good communication is kept up between the pastor and the lay pastoral caregiver. **All written records should be kept in confidentiality.** This may also be used as a reporting mechanism.

Monthly Training Meetings

In addition to the initial training weekend, caregivers commit to attending monthly training sessions during their one-year commitment to study more extensively the topics in Part III and to discuss situations in which they feel uncomfortable and need some guidance. It is essential that the lay pastoral caregivers *not* use the names of the people to whom they are assigned during their group meetings! Confidentiality is the cornerstone of any program of this nature; such a concern for privacy and confidentiality cannot be overstressed. At the same time, sharing concerns, problems encountered, and possible solutions can be very beneficial for everyone.

Each month when the lay pastoral caregivers meet, another chapter is introduced for in-depth study. The meeting should be led by the pastor and begin with prayer for the lay pastors and those to whom they minister. After the chapter material is presented, there should be a time for questions about how best to handle a particular situation. The lay pastoral caregivers are never to use the names of the people to whom they are assigned and conversations about all situations are to remain confidential.

A suggested evening meeting outline might be:

- 7:30-7:40 Gathering with refreshments
- 7:40-7:50 Devotional time led by the pastor or volunteers.
- 7:50-8:40 Introduction of new chapter material from Part III
- 8:40-9:00 Time for questions and review assignments for the coming month
- 9:00   Prayer and adjournment

Celebrating and Supporting the Caregivers

After the group has finished the basic training, the congregation should celebrate the group's accomplishment with a commissioning or consecration service (suggested format appears later in this chapter). Such a celebration will help everyone understand the program and how the church will benefit from it. This is an opportunity for the pastor to preach on one of the texts in the first chapter, particularly the Ephesians text, to explain how important this new program is to the life of the congregation and to the overall understanding of the ministry of the laity. You may also choose to use a church newsletter or website to highlight the new program. Take pictures of the new lay pastoral caregivers and post them in a well-traveled location along with an explanation of this new ministry.

The commissioning of lay caregivers happens with the regular service of worship. The public nature of the ceremony is important for the lay pastoral caregivers, for the congregation, and for newcomers to the church. For those who are commissioned, the service becomes a source of power and support. For the congregation, the commissioning informs and stimulates a prayerful concern for the work of the lay pastoral caregivers. Newcomers and established church members will gain insight into the church's understanding of the ministry of the laity and the equipping of disciples for ministry through the work of the Holy Spirit.

This kind of service is a testimony to our interdependence on one another as brothers and sisters in Christ, both lay and clergy to doing all we can to help establish the Kingdom. Its theological grounding comes from the Great Commission. (Matthew 28: 19-20) These verses assured the first disciples that Jesus would be with them as they performed their work. For us these verses mean that we believe God will be with us as we work on behalf of God, doing God's will, assisting our brothers and sisters in need.

Sample Commissioning Service

Pastor: Brothers and sisters in Christ, the people who stand before you have answered a call to become lay pastoral caregivers. They have received training in the skills necessary to carry out their assignments under pastoral supervision, and have committed to continue to meet monthly for additional training throughout the year. They will assist me in providing pastoral care to you. They are equipped to listen to your concerns, to pray for you, and to assist you in various ways. Strengthened by the Holy Spirit and girded by prayer and faith, they are prepared to provide pastoral care.

Lay pastoral caregivers, do you promise to continue faithfully your participation in the monthly training and all of the other expectations of this program for one year?

Response: I do.

Pastor: Will you perform your duties in such a way as to insure confidentiality?

Response: I will.

Pastor: Will you use the pastoral tools of prayer, Scripture, Eucharist, and listening in the performance of your duties?

Response: I will.

Pastor: Members of the congregation, will you support these before you in their ministry to you and accept them as part of the pastoral ministry of this congregation?

Response: We will. We pray God's blessing upon them in this ministry to which they have been called.

Pastor or other leader of church then offers the following prayer:

Creator God, give us a heart that is open to new possibilities. We are grateful for servants who are willing to serve you as lay pastoral caregivers. We pray your blessing upon them in this new ministry. By your Spirit, guide them and help them to do your will. We pray in Jesus' name. Amen.

Additional Resources:

The United Methodist Hymnal and *The United Methodist Book of Worship* may be helpful in creating a commissioning service.

Chapter Two Review

1. List the steps of the lay pastoral care giving program.
2. How will a verbatim account of a visit help you? What do you imagine you will learn when others read an account of a visit to another person? How might this experience help you reflect the caring ministry of Jesus Christ?
3. Why do you think confidentiality is needed for this program?

PART II

Preparation for Caring Ministry

CHAPTER THREE

Making an Appointment, Keeping the Appointment, and Reporting on the Appointment

Making an Appointment

After the initial training is complete, the pastor will assign each lay pastoral caregiver a person to contact. The purpose of this initial contact is to explain in brief the role of the lay caregiver in relationship to the person assigned. The following is an outline of that first phone call:

1. Call and identifies yourself by name and explain your connection with the church. At this point it is important to get permission to continue with the conversation, so a question such as "Is this a good time to talk?" or "Do you have time to talk to me?" is quite appropriate. If the answer is no, try to set a time for another telephone conversation.

2. If permission is given to continue the conversation, explain your understanding of the ministry of a lay pastoral caregiver. After such an explanation, a statement such as "Rev. XYZ asked me to bring communion elements to you and I told him that I would be happy to do so" is enough information to start a deeper conversation. There may be some resistance, and you should try to deal with this without argument and by being as accommodating as possible. If the parishioner does not want a visit, you should notify the pastor.

3. You should clearly communicate that you are caregiver from the church and that you are visiting as part of the congregation's ministry. If it is possible, be brief as you explain the purpose of lay pastoral care giving. If you wish to say more about your sense of God's love and caring, you may wish to wait for an appropriate moment in the conversation.

4. Once the introductory part of the conversation is over, it is time to get some information from the parishioner. Prior to the call, the pastor will give you the name, phone number, address, and reason for the pastoral care assignment, but any other additional information will come in this phone conversation.

5. You should ask questions to help clarify where the person lives or to get directions to the person's residence.

6. Now you should arrange a date for the first visit, establishing by mutual agreement the time and the length of the visit. You may say something like "I think we can make this first visit relatively short. Would a 30-minute visit suit your schedule?" This gives the parishioner some assurance that they will not be stuck with a relative stranger in their home for an unlimited time.

7. Before concluding the phone call, take time to review together and confirm the date, time, place, length of stay, and directions to the residence.

Keeping the Appointment

Because of the need for the lay pastoral caregiver and the parishioner to start well, it is imperative that this first appointment be kept as agreed. Plan to allow some extra time to get to the home in case traffic is bad or the directions are inexact. If delay seems possible, call the parishioner to explain the situation.

When the lay pastoral caregiver does get to the home of the parishioner, he or she should wait for an invitation to sit. Good advice is to sit only where and when invited. Some people have favorite chairs they prefer to sit in. If no specific chair is indicated, the lay pastoral caregiver should sit so that everyone in the room is visible. It is important to establish and maintain good eye contact during the conversation. Once the lay pastoral care-giver establishes again the intent of the visit, it is also important to state the amount of time agreed on for the visit. Once this is completed, make note of the room and any special photos or figurines that might be used as a conversation starter and a way to connect with the parishioner. Sometimes "small talk" can put people at ease. After this introduction, it is time for the lay pastoral caregiver to get down to business. Their business is one of listening; to do so the caregiver may need to explain once again what his/her role is in the life of the congregation. Once the parishioner is at ease, he/she may begin to share stories and feelings. By listening carefully, the lay pastoral caregiver can give tremendous assistance to the parishioner by offering a sounding board, feedback, a fresh perspective on any issue and on matters of faith. It is essential that the lay pastoral caregiver give all of his or her attention to the parishioner during the visits to encourage the other person to talk about issues that may be on the parishioner's mind. The lay pastoral caregiver should also listen with the intent to remember the conversation and write a verbatim about the visit as soon as he/she gets back to the car. When the agreed-upon time has come, the lay pastoral caregiver should indicate to the parishioner that it is time to conclude the visit. If appropriate, the lay pastoral caregiver should try to schedule another mutually agreed-upon visit. Always offer to pray with the parishioner before leaving.

Most lay pastoral care visits will take place in a residence. Sometimes a lay pastoral caregiver may visit someone in a hospital or a long-term care facility. It is important that the lay pastoral caregiver feel comfortable in these settings and it is also important that they understand reasons the parishioner is in such a setting. The first advice therefore is to keep the visits to people in institutional settings brief; not more than 30 minutes, and usually less. Remember that people in institutional settings are sometimes on special diets, and treats such as homemade cookies may not be welcome. Likewise flowers from the back yard might seem like a nice gesture, except that many people have allergies. On the other hand, notes or cards signed by the members of a Sunday School class or other church members are always welcome.

When visiting in a hospital, the lay pastoral caregiver should:

1. Be aware of the visiting hours.
2. Call ahead to see if the parishioner would like a visit and if they have any tests or procedures scheduled for any particular time.
3. Stop at the front desk to get the room number if the pastor has not provided it.
4. Knock on the door and ask if it is OK to visit at this time. If hospital staff members are in the room, wait outside until they have finished.
5. Note the details when entering the room to see if there are cards or flowers or special equipment in use.
6. Try to determine if it is more comfortable for the parishioner to look at you while you stand or sit.
7. Stand or sit where the parishioner can easily see and hear you. Hospitals have their own noises. Stand or sit close enough to hear and be heard.
8. During the visit be sensitive to clues that the parishioner may be uncomfortable or in pain.
9. Do not inquire about the illness, only about how the parishioner feels. If the parishioner want to share more, he or she will.
10. In the event the parishioner asks for anything, always ask the staff if it is OK to give it to the person. Do not adjust the bed height or give a drink of water without approval from the medical team because of the potential interference with a procedure or test.
11. Make the visit brief (30 minutes or less).
12. Offer a prayer or Bible reading that is supportive and uplifting.

When visiting in a nursing home, the lay pastoral caregiver should:

1. Call ahead to make an appointment to visit.
2. Stop at the main desk to sign in and get the appropriate room number.
3. Knock at the door and ask if it is OK to enter. If nursing home staff members are present, wait in the hallway until they have finished.
4. Note the details of the room to see if there are family pictures, special furniture or framed awards that might lead to discussion.
5. Ask the parishioner where to stand or sit for the visit.
6. Be aware that many elderly do not hear very well.

7. In the event the parishioner asks for anything, always ask the staff if it is OK to give it to the person.

Writing a Verbatim

After the visit, the lay pastoral caregiver should write out as much as possible what was said. Begin with an outline of topics included in the conversation. For instance, the outline might say:

- Introduced self
- Commented on picture (was deceased husband Ralph)
- Discussed support received during funeral
- Shared how lonely she is now.
- I invited her to our grief support group.
- She changed subject
- We had a prayer and I left.

After the outline is complete, the lay pastoral caregiver should go back and complete this outline with whole sentences and as much of the conversation as they can recall around each of the major points. Review the visit mentally and try to make the verbatim as accurate as possible. Use abbreviations such as LP for Lay Pastoral Caregiver and the initials of the person visited. The finished verbatim should have an introduction that includes the name of the person visited, the purpose for the visit, the place of the visit, any impressions the lay pastoral caregiver had from viewing the surroundings, and the mood of the parishioner. After the introduction is complete, the verbatim of the conversation comes next. Conclude the verbatim with reflection on how the lay pastoral caregiver felt about the visit and other specific impressions and concerns.

Think of the verbatim as a teaching tool to improve listening gifts and to respond more appropriately. It should be typed and returned to the pastor for his or her review. After the pastor reviews it, he or she will spend some one-on-one time helping point out how the next visit might go better.

Providing pastoral care is a sacred trust. Sharing what was said during a visit with anyone but the pastor violates that trust—unless complaints of abusive behavior come out in the conversation, in which case, notify your pastor and/or the nurse of your concern. All written material must be handled with the highest security. At monthly meetings, sharing circumstances or parts of conversations is appropriate, but, as has been mentioned previously, any shared conversations regarding lay pastoral visits should be kept in confidence.

Chapter Three Review

1. What is the procedure for making a call and making a visit? Why is the initial contact important?
2. What are the steps for writing a verbatim? What is the purpose of writing a verbatim after each visit?

CHAPTER FOUR

Pastoral Tools

Every profession has a toolbox full of the things that are necessary for the person in that profession to do their work. For clergy, this toolbox includes prayer, the Bible, the sacraments, and the ability to listen. These same tools are also appropriate for the lay pastoral caregiver.

Prayer

Each lay pastoral caregiver meeting, including the initial training program, should begin with prayer. Pray for each caregiver and those to whom the group will extend care. Ask God to work through them and pray that the lay pastoral caregivers will be open to the leading of the Holy Spirit.

Encourage the lay pastoral caregivers to follow a simple pattern of praying for those to whom they are assigned.

- Pray for God's guidance just before going into the parishioner's home.
- As the visit ends, ask the parishioner about any particular needs and offer to pray with them for these needs. Place the needs before God with the firm conviction that the will of God will be done.
- When the lay pastoral caregiver leaves the residence, it is appropriate to thank God for the guidance and strength given to provide this ministry.

If appropriate, after consultations with the pastor, the names of those who would like prayer should be submitted to the church's intercessory prayer group, if the congregation has one. If not, it is appropriate for the lay pastoral caregiver to keep a list of his/her own people for whom they should pray on a regular basis.

Prayer is an essential tool in this ministry. Praying aloud with others may not be something that the lay pastoral caregivers are accustomed to doing, but with practice these steps will feel natural. All will benefit from the closer relationship to God that will result from these prayer practices.

Scripture

Some people say that you can find justification for nearly action simply by pointing to it somewhere in the Bible. To some degree, that is true. The Bible is full of real life stories about real life people who have real life problems and temptations. The lessons these people learned and the teachings of Jesus regarding love of neighbor and those of Paul regarding God's grace are appropriate to share with people who are facing similar situations today. The lay pastoral caregiver should never use Scripture to beat up people or punish them, but to encourage them as they face struggles. When a visit is scheduled, take a Bible and be prepared to read aloud a Bible verse or short Bible passage that offers encouragement in times of need. Many people memorize such verses, and those visited may be able to repeat the words with the lay pastoral caregiver. This is especially true with individuals who are elderly. The lay pastoral caregiver could ask the parishioner if they have requests or a particular passage of Scripture that they would like read. A Bible with a compact concordance section helps to find verses that deal with topics such grace, forgiveness, love, or peace. It is not necessary to be a biblical scholar to open the Bible and discover God's grace.

Eucharist

Many churches allow laity to take the communion elements to the shut-ins once they have been consecrated in the Eucharist service. Sharing these elements, along with brief statements like, "The bread symbolizes the body of our Lord Jesus Christ given for you," and "The cup symbolizes the blood of our Lord Jesus Christ shed for you," will help the shut-in feel like they are connected with the local congregation. If the lay pastoral caregiver *does* take the communion elements to their parishioner, it is best to do so as soon after the service as possible. To enhance the sense of being a part of the worshiping body, it would be good to take along a bulletin and perhaps an audio or video tape of the service to listen to with the shut in. By sharing that part of the service where the confession is made and the elements consecrated, they will certainly feel like they have participated in the sacrament. It may be a good idea for the lay pastoral caregiver to take along a hymnal so that the parishioner can read along with the communion liturgy. This kind of participation can only help to keep the parishioner, who is unable to attend worship for whatever reason, connected to the congregation. Mark W. Stamm in *Extending the Table: A Guide for a Ministry of Home Communion Serving* (Discipleship Resources, 2009) offers a theological understanding of home visits with Holy Communion and also offers some practical ideas.

Listening

Being a good listener is perhaps the most important tool of the lay pastoral caregiver. It defines the role. In *The Seven Habits of Highly Effective People*, Stephen Covey lists "Seek first to understand, then to be understood" as a key habit. This excellent advice encourages lay pastoral caregivers always to listen first and offer suggestions or advice last. Be always mindful of the folk wisdom that God gave us two ears and only one mouth, thus making it possible to listen twice as much as we talk. By listening, lay pastoral caregivers will better understand what the person they are assigned to thinks, feels, and needs. Communication is both passing along and receiving information. We receive information by listening, reading, and observing. All of what we receive is filtered by our own backgrounds, needs, interpretation, and agendas. Two people may hear the same information and respond to it differently. The lay pastoral caregiver must be aware of his or her own filters (see sidebar) and be aware that when he or she is passing along information, the recipients of the information will also filter it.

There is a difference between hearing and active listening. *Hearing* is the physical process of having sound waves vibrate against the eardrums, and then processing that sound wave into the vibrations of fluid within the inner ear where it propagates mechanical signals from the middle ear as waves in fluid and membranes, and then transduces them to nerve impulses which are transmitted to the brain. Active *listening* is when we try to understand what the other person is saying. It involves paying attention.

The following steps can help improve our listening skills:

- Show attentiveness by facing the speaker.
- Show interest by maintaining eye contact with the speaker at least 80% of the time.
- Avoid prejudging the worthiness of the message based on the age of the person, his/her appearance, etc.
- Listen to the intent of what the speaker is saying.
- Avoid tuning out to prepare your response while the other is still speaking.
- Ask question to clarify what was said.
- Avoid interrupting the speaker.
- Avoid trying to have the last word.

Personality tests can help us understand differences among individuals. According to Myers-Briggs Type Indicator, there are four areas of personality that show opposite styles. Why go to the trouble of taking the test? Knowing where you fit into these four categories will help you understand how you receive information.

Extrovert or Introvert? The extrovert processes information externally—by talking. They enjoy being with other people, are happy in large groups, and are eager to talk. If you are extroverted, you will want to talk about what has been shared with you. Chances are you will ask questions of clarifications, or even share a story of an event in your own life that was similar to what had just been told you. The introvert, on the other hand, processes information internally. They like to be by themselves, prefer to work in small groups, and appear reluctant to share their thoughts. If you are introverted, you may receive information, say thank you and go on with your day processing internally what was said, why it was said, how it was said, and what it might mean.

Intuitive or Sensing? A sensing person seems to be interested in the details, what can be learned from seeing, tasting, hearing, feeling, and smelling. They enjoy the process of getting from step one to step ten even more than the result. The sensing person will follow the plan and enjoy the procedure, but may not be very good at making the plan in the first place. If you are a sensing person you may hear something and want to know more about the information, how it was attained, how accurate it was, and how to move on from what had been communicated. On the other hand, the intuitive person sees the big picture and envisions goals and missions. They love to be the starters and leave the implementation up to the sensing people. The intuitive person may hear the same information and begin to see plans for getting started with a solution.

Thinking or Feeling? Feeling people are interested in relationships, values, and fairness. They often decide things on an emotion. The feeling person may be concerned about how what has been communicated might seem fair or unfair to themselves or others hearing the same information. They may not like what they are hearing, but for the sake of a good relationship, accept it. Thinking people, by contrast, are more analytical. They want to know the rules and how to follow them. The thinking person may hear something and begin to set parameters of what would be an acceptable response.

Perceiving or Judging? The perceiving person gets together data from a variety of sources, processes it, decides, and then may gather more information to re-process a decision. The perceiving person may be able to receive information from one source and listen to comments from a variety of others before coming up with a comment that pulls discussion together and enables a group to move onto the next step. The judging person wants to make quick decisions, is interested in getting it done and moving on. They tend to work best with a list they can check off, and enjoy order rather than confusion. The judging person may hear something and instantly decide if they accept it or not or what their response needs to be.

Listening is a major part of communication. But we are all different, and we receive and pass along information differently. In addition, we all come with our histories, or filters, that determine how we hear what we hear. We may listen less intently to a man as opposed to a woman or a young person as opposed to an older person.

In a seminar I attended on stress, one leader said that, when pushed by stress or crises, people are like skunks or turtles. "Skunky" people are those who blame everyone else when under stress. They spray all over the place, blaming everyone but himself or herself. People who are like turtles, when stressed, blame themselves. They withdraw and beat themselves up over things that may not be their fault. It is easy to pick out the skunks and turtles. The people to whom lay pastoral caregivers are assigned will, in the extreme, be one or the other. Knowing this is the case, it may be a little easier when someone the lay pastoral caregiver visits blasts him or her. It works best to simply understand that this person is a "skunk."

Levels of Communication

Communication has within it several levels. It is important to understand these levels as we deal with others. Occasionally, the lay pastoral caregiver maybe be assigned to someone who is upset with the church or pastor or God. If this is the case, when the person is expressing his/her anger, try to sort through the words used to determine what facts are being presented. Do not try to defend the church, pastor, or God. Do, however, listen intently for the facts that are being presented. Understand that getting the facts from one person is like asking five people who are blindfolded to describe an elephant. The person who feels a leg will describe the leg. The person who feels the tail will describe a tail. Likewise, the people feeling the trunk and ears will describe what they believe to be the facts. It is important to hear from as many people as possible about an incident before making a decision as to what actually happened and how to deal with it.

On a second level, people who talk to lay pastoral caregivers will be expressing not simply the facts, which is what is essential for understanding a problem, but also opinions. Opinions are offered after someone has reviewed the facts. They see or hear something and come to a conclusion, which is an opinion. For instance the person talking to the lay pastoral caregiver may say that worship attendance has been down lately. That may be a fact. Then they may add, "That new minister is not a very good preacher." This is an opinion. Try to separate facts from opinions by asking clarifying questions. Determine what is true from what is perceived. Once the facts are ascertained, it is possible to deal with the opinions expressed. The lay pastoral caregiver might say, "Tell me more about why you think that." A simple, "Thank you for your opinion," would carry the same message.

A third level of communication is feeling or emotions. Oftentimes conversations can be emotional. People may express anger or sadness as they communicate with the lay pastoral caregiver. Once the facts and opinions are weeded out, it is important to understand that emotions may be the driving force for the conversation in the first place. Sentences that begin with "I feel . . ." are expressions of emotion. The person may say, "I feel angry that the Bishop has stuck us with such a poor preacher. Our poor little church will never recover." The fact is that attendance is down. The opinion is that this is the case because the minister is a poor preacher. And the emotion expressed is anger at the Bishop because he/she appointed the minister to the church. The steps discussed above will help clarify what actually happened. Weed out the facts. Is the attendance down? What reasons might there be for this fact? Deal with the opinion the poor preaching by discussing all facets of worship, potential good points to sermons you have heard. And finally, deal with the emotion expressed. In this case, the person is angry and you are the one getting the blast. The lay pastoral caregiver should try to not respond in anger or defense. Let the other person express him or herself. When they are through, deal with the emotion. Something like, "I understand that you are upset about the steady decline of our church," will enable the person to talk some more about their feelings. It is better to have them sharing with the lay pastoral caregiver than non-members who live in the neighborhood. Everybody feels better if someone else listens to him or her express his/her emotion. But it is essential that once the emotion is expressed, there is some sort of agreement on what will be done. In some cases we can only validate their feelings without agreeing. In other cases we may be able to do something to make them feel better or to remedy the situation. Communication is a little like getting to know someone on a first date. Facts are shared easily, like what someone likes or where they have lived, or perhaps, their occupation. At some point, conversations may go a step deeper and involve an opinion about a city or a sports team or a profession. As people become comfortable with one another, they may share an emotion, a fear, anger, and a joy. Emotions like fear or joy are normally shared after people feel comfortable talking with each other. Responding to an emotion with words that tell the other person you understand them and are concerned for them will enable them to share more of the same. To insure that the church member will feel comfortable sharing with you requires that the lay pastoral caregiver spends time listening to their concerns.

Verbal, Nonverbal, and Written Communication

We communicate in many forms. The three most obvious are the verbal, the nonverbal, and the written. The verbal type of communication is what we say. This seems pretty straightforward. But, there are many ways to say things that create different meanings. If someone says, "Where did you get that outfit?" the meaning of the question may depend the tone used to ask the question. It could be a compliment if the voice is higher and full of enthusiasm. Or it could be a snide remark if asked with a bit of a sneer. Or it could simply be a direct question. How we say what we say determines what others interpret our meaning to be. Sarcasm is a way of saying something using words that may appear to be positive but saying them in such a way as to imply just the opposite. Verbal communication can be misleading and not so direct.

Nonverbal communication is simply communicating without saying anything. The classic example of non-verbal communication is crossed arms or legs. These normally imply that the person is not receptive to listening to what you have to say. Open arms and leaning toward the speaker implies that there is interest in what is being said. Making a statement followed by touching ones nose normally implies that the person is not telling the truth. A look between friends can communicate, "Did you hear that?" or "I told you she would say that." A raised eyebrow could imply some doubt. A frown expresses disappointment or disapproval. Raising your eyes may indicate that you are thinking about something. A furrowed brow may indicate that one is thinking about what was just said. Smiles normally imply that everything is fine.

As a lay pastoral caregiver, the goal is to build open communication with the church member to whom you are assigned. Gestures, posture, and facial expressions are all aspects of body language that can encourage open communication and support your spoken message. As mentioned above, a smile can be disarming and can set the tone for open communication. Making eye contact at least 80% of the time also shows positive interest in the other person.

Written communication is perhaps the most direct because it requires that you say what you mean. Emails these days are often quick responses that get right to the point. Letters tend to require more thought and normally require better grammar.

Understanding that people will communicate in various ways and send and receive information in various ways will help with misunderstandings in the future. It is always best if you are not sure what is being said to simply ask for clarification rather than assume you understand.

Lay pastoral caregivers will occasionally be assigned to work with an elderly member of the congregation. It is important to understand that communication with an older person carries with it some extra obstacles. Some degree of impaired vision and hearing is common with most people who are elderly. When speaking to one of these older people, try doing some of the following:

- Stand or sit in front of the person and if possible, at their eye level, so they are aware that you are there and can focus their attention upon you.
- Gently touch the older person to get their attention before you begin to speak.
- Call the older person by name before you begin to speak.
- If the person is hearing impaired, make sure they can see your face, and especially your mouth, as you speak.
- Speak slowly and clearly.
- Many hearing impaired people are able to hear lower tones easier than higher tones. Try to use a lower voice when speaking to them.
- Use gestures to help demonstrate your point.
- Give the older person time to respond before moving on to the next question.

Being a good communicator is essential if one is to be a good lay pastoral caregiver. Listening carefully to what others are saying is the first step in communication. It may be the most important of all the "pastoral tools."

Additional Resources:

Messages: The Communications Skills Book, by Matthew McKay, Martha Davis and Patrick Fanning (New Harbinger Publications, 1995)

101 Ways to Improve Your Communication Skills Instantly, by Bennie Bough (GoalMinds, 2008)

Understanding Human Communication, by Ronald B. Adler and George Rodman (Oxford University Press, 2005)

Interpersonal Communication Book the 11th edition, by Joseph A. DeVito (Allyn & Bacon 2005)

The United Methodist Hymnal

The Holy Bible

Chapter Four Review

1. What prayer steps are listed in the chapter? How maythey may assist you in becoming better attuned to God?
2. What passages of Scripture verses encourage and help you in times of trouble? Take time to reread this passages as you remember them.
3. What information does a concordance give about the Bible?
4. Put yourself in the place of someone who is unable to come to worship. Imagine what they would like the church to do for or with them. Discuss this situation with others in the group.
5. Why it is important to become a good listener?
6. Strike up a brief conversation with someone. At its conclusion, write a practice verbatim of the conversation.
7. Write out a short story from your past and go over it to identify the facts, the opinions and the feelings in the story.
8. What were the points involved in active listening.
9. Give examples of verbal, non-verbal and written communication. What are the advantages and disadvantages of each?

CHAPTER FIVE

Developmental Understandings Relevant to Pastoral Care

This chapter presents information concerning basic understandings of human development. We look first at the human development theory as understood and presented by Erik Erikson. Erikson's understanding of development serves as our foundation for understanding life stages. Then we will look at Gail Sheehy's popular and accurate information regarding movement through the stages of life. After that we will examine the theory of faith development as presented by James Fowler. By referencing the work of these three innovative thinkers, I hope to help the lay pastoral caregivers establish a good foundational understanding of people and their various needs.

Ego Development

Erik Erikson was a well-known psychologist who studied at the Vienna Psychoanalytic Institute. Erikson published his life-cycle theory in 1950 in a book entitled *Childhood and Society*. Here he laid out his "eight ages" of humanity. These eight ages are also called eight stages of ego development. This brief summary of those stages will enable those who are training to be lay pastoral caregivers to be aware of one theory of human development, but I offer only the most basic introduction. Erikson's work is still published and studied by many. By understanding these stages of development, the lay pastoral caregiver will understand various stages of the lives of those for whom they care. Most often they will be assigned to adults and in many cases, older adults, but occasionally children or adolescents may need special attention and care.

Human development, according to Erikson, proceeds by stages. People move from stage to stage until they have reached the final stage. Good progress at one stage enhances the possibility of good progress at the next; however, if one gets bogged down at one stage , it does not mean the person will falter in the next developmental stage. One of the things Erickson emphasizes is that as people move from one stage to the next, they leave the previous stage behind chronologically, but not psychologically. Each stage in human development exerts an influence upon us that will influence us for the rest of our lives. Recognize that every human progresses from one stage to the next. One stage builds upon another.

Having a sense of the developmental stages will also help us understand attitudes people have toward other people and community. The developmental stages also influence the images people have of God. Having a basic understanding of Erikson's stages will help us focus on other life concerns. These will give us a foundation for understanding our caring for others and will help us develop an awareness of our deeper compassion.

Stage 1: Trust vs. Mistrust

Is the world loving and kind? Does it support and sustain us? Does the world provide for our needs? Does God love us? These questions are answered through the experiences we have in this first stage of life. Are the needs of the infant met or is the infant regularly neglected? Because the infant is helpless to care for his or her needs, the infant depends on and trusts others for that care. Basic trust develops during the first year of life. When the infant does not receive such care, an estrangement happens. This estrangement may characterize individuals who withdraw into themselves or who refuse to participate with others because they don't trust. Trust becomes the basis for our capacity for faith. Some theologians in the area of pastoral care point to this stage of life as the most important time when humans develop their capacity for faith in God.

Stage 2: Autonomy vs. Shame and Doubt

One- to three-year-olds can express their own independent will. That is not a surprising statement to anyone who has lived with young children. On the one hand they want to do it themselves; on the other hand, they begin to believe that other people cannot make them do something they do not want to do. When subjected to excessive shaming, the child tends to develop great inner rage or anger toward the person doing the shaming. Because of what happens in this stage of development, shame and self-doubt will show up through the rest of the life cycle as low self-esteem.

Stage 3: Initiative vs. Guilt

Between the ages of three and six, children begin to exert control over their environment. For example, they make decisions about their activities. Children who succeed in this stage develop a sense of purpose. Children who seek to exert too much power in attempts to control this environment may experience parental disapproval, which results in feelings of guilt. As with shame in the earlier stage, guilt at this stage will show up throughout the life cycle as low self-esteem.

Stage 4: Industry vs. Inferiority

From ages six to 11, children begin the journey of education in our school systems. Industry involves doing things beside and with others. They face many expectations and demands. Success brings a sense of competence.

Failure brings feelings of inferiority, and an individual may take many years to overcome these feelings

Stage 5: Identity vs. Role Confusion

Adolescents need to develop a sense of self and personal identity. We see this in the experimentation that comes with the teenage years. Successful personal identity leads to an ability to stay true to oneself, while failure may lead to role confusion and a weak sense of self. Fidelity and loyalty are key developments at this stage, and we see these attributes in matters of faith.

Stage 6: Intimacy vs. Isolation

With young adulthood comes a need to form intimate, loving relationships with other people. (This stage ranges from ages 19-40, depending on the individual.) Success leads to strong relationships and deep friendships. Partnerships develop. Failure in this stage may result in loneliness and isolation.

Stage 7 :Generatively vs. Stagnation

Generatively is the concern for establishing and guiding the next generation; it is the task of mid-life. Adults need to create or nurture things that will outlast them. We have children or we create some positive change for the benefit of other people. Success leads to feelings of usefulness, Success at this stage of generativity grows from the faith, will, purpose, and competence that Erikson points to in the first four stages of life.

Stage 8: Integrity vs. Disgust

In the aging person who has taken care of life and has adapted to the triumphs and disappointments of existence, the fruit of the seven stages gradually ripens. Erikson called this fruit integrity. We gain an assurance of order and meaning—an emotional integration faithful to the past and ready to take leadership in the present. Another word for this may be wisdom. At this stage of life, we look back at life and feel a sense of fulfillment. The opposite of such development may bring feelings of regret, bitterness, and despair.[1]

Consider this the most basic summary of Erikson's theory. If you have time and interest, plan to read *Childhood and Society*.

Essential Life Passages

Where Erikson left off his study of adulthood, Gail Sheehy picked up in her book *Passages*. Sheehy says, "If one sees the personality not as an apparatus that is essentially constructed by the time childhood is over, but as always in its essence developing, then life at 25 or 30 or at the gateway to middle age will stimulate its own intrigue, surprise and exhilaration of discovery."[2]

Sheehy compares the moving from one stage to another to the process of a lobster growing and shedding its prior shell.

> With each passage from one stage of human growth to the next we, too, must shed a protective structure. We are left exposed and vulnerable-but also yeasty and embryonic again, capable of stretching in ways we hadn't known before. These shedding may take several years or more. Coming out of each passage, though, we enter a longer and more stable period in which we can expect relative tranquility and a sense of equilibrium regained.[3]

The moves from one place to another, the passages, are a time of crises and disruption, and may take many years. They force us to move from our comfortable places in life to grow into another stage. Further, some crises of adulthood are predictable.

> Everything that happens to us—graduations, marriage, childbirth, divorce, getting or losing a job—affects us. These *marker events* are the concrete happenings of our lives. A developmental stage, however, is not defined in terms or marker events; it is defined by changes that begin

within. *The underlying impulse toward change will be there regardless* of whether or not it is manifested in our accentuated by a marker event.[4]

During this time of transition, we may feel out of sorts. Sheehy says that how we feel about our way of living will undergo subtle changes in four areas of perception. The four areas are the interior sense of self in relation to others; the proportion of safeness to danger we feel; our perception of time (do we have plenty of it or is our time running out?); a gut level sense of a shift in our aliveness or stagnation.[5] When we are aware of these feelings, most often we begin to do something to make ourselves feel more comfortable again.

While no "life cycle" will be appropriate for all people over all generations, what Sheehy has offered in *Passages* and *New Passages* depict periods and passages that most people go through as they age. Knowing these passages will help the lay pastoral caregiver understand what a parishioner may be experiencing.

Pulling Up Roots

Before 18, the motto is, "I have to get away from my parents." But the teen seldom acts on the words. If these young people go away to college or join the military or simply go out on their own, they feel their autonomy growing and the passage of pulling up roots begins. This is the time to test out what the young person believes about God, politics, morals, and ethics. They no longer have their parents to review every comment or decision. Contemporaries replace the allies their parents used to be so long as their new young adult perspectives mesh.

The task of this passage is to find a peer group role, a sex role, an anticipated occupation role, an ideology, or a worldview. When they do, they are able to begin to leave home emotionally.

The Trying Twenties

During this passage, one is confronted with how to function in an adult world. During these years one is preoccupied with how to put aspirations into effect, where to begin, and who can be of assistance.

The tasks of this period are to shape a dream, to prepare for a life-work, to find a mentor, and to form the capacity for intimacy without losing whatever consistency of self one has generated thus far.

This is a time when one does what he or she "should" do. The agenda for twenty-somethings: get a job, find a life partner, and settle down. Sheehy also tells us that there are two urges in this period. The first is to build a firm, safe structure for the future and the second is to explore and experiment, keeping any structure tentative.[6]

Catch 30

As men and women approach their 30s, they often talk about feeling too narrow or restricted. Choices made in their 20s now seem to be inappropriate. A common response is to tear up the life one spent most of one's 20s putting together and change gears, moving toward a new vision, a new dream, perhaps a more realistic dream. This review of things previously held as important may include a marriage just as easily as a career.

Rooting and Expanding

Life becomes more rational and orderly in the early 30s. This is the time to put down roots, to buy homes, and to become sincere corporate ladder climbers. Men tend to become more concerned about their careers and their marriage is sacrificed often to obtain this goal. The social life of the 20s has changed because now there may be children, and have needs that require adult attention.

The Deadline Decade

In the middle 30s, one begins to see the end of a career. They begin to realize that they are no longer "young." They are approaching middle age. This is the age of faltering physical powers, and the realization that one does not have all of the spiritual answers. This decade is the time to reexamine one's purpose and reevaluate one's priority for using resources. Often times it is during this time frame of 35 to 45 that men and women begin to assert themselves because they have taken stock and determined that life is too short and they need to do some things that they have not done thus far. Often times it is during this mid-life that men feel stale, restless, burdened, and unappreciated. As a result, some men seek second carreers while others become self-destructive.

Renewal or Resignation

If one has confronted oneself in the middle passage and found a renewal of purpose around which to build an authentic life structure, these latter years of adulthood can be the best years. At 50 there can be new warmth and mellowing. Friends and privacy become more important than ever. This is a time for frankness and honesty with oneself and others.[7]

Sheehy recently noted a revolution in the above life cycle, and wrote about it in *New Passages*:

> There is a revolution in the life cycle. In the space of one short generation the whole shape of the life cycle has been fundamentally altered. People today are leaving childhood sooner, but they are taking longer to grow up and much longer to die. Puberty arrives earlier by several years than it did at the turn of the century. Adolescence is now prolonged for the middle class until the end of the twenties and for blue-collar men and women until the mid-twenties, as more young adults live at home longer. True adulthood doesn't begin until 30. Most Baby Boomers, born after World War II, do not feel fully "grown up" until they are into their forties, and even then they resist.
>
> Middle age has already been pushed far into the fifties-if it is acknowledged at all today. The territory of the fifties, sixties, and beyond is changing so radically that it now opens up whole new passages leading to stages of life that are nothing like what our parents or grandparents experienced. Fifty is now what 40 used to be.[8]

Faith Development

James Fowler wrote extensively on the area of faith development, and is acknowledged by some scholars as the founder of faith development theory. Based on Erickson's developmental understanding, the work of child psychologist Jean Piaget, and the moral theory of Lawrence Kohlberg, Fowler identifies six stages of faith.

Stage One: Intuitive-Projective Faith (Ages 3-7)

This stage is marked by constant stimulation and fluid thought patterns. The child is continually encountering novelties for which no stable operations of knowing have been formed. This stage is a fantasy-filled imitative phase in which the child can be powerfully and permanently influenced by examples, moods, actions, and stories of the visible faith of primarily related adults. This stage produces long-lasting images and feelings (both positive and negative). Later on, more stable and self-reflective valuing and thinking will have to order and sort these images out.

The gift or strength of this stage is the birth of imagination, the ability to unify and grasp the world of everyday experience in powerful images and as presented in stories that register the child's intuitive understandings and feelings toward the ultimate conditions of existence.

The dangers in this stage arise from the possible "possession" of the child's imagination by unrestrained images of terror and destructiveness, or from the witting and unwitting exploitation of her or his imagination in the reinforcement of taboos and moral or doctrinal expectations. This stage produces children who are legalistic and moral, never wavering from black or white, or good or bad. They can develop an "us against them" mentality with "us" being correct in all things.

The main factor precipitating transition to the next stage is the emergence of concrete operational thinking, which typically appears around age six. At the heart of the transition is the child's growing concern to know how things are and to clarify for him- or herself the bases of distinctions between what is real and what is not.

Stage Two: Mythical-Literal Faith (School Age)

The new capacity or strength in this stage is the rise of narrative, and the emergence of story, drama, and myth as ways of finding and giving coherence to experience. Story becomes the major way of giving unity and value to experience. Those in Stage Two can be affected deeply and powerfully by symbolic and dramatic materials, and can describe in endlessly detailed narrative what has occurred. They are not ready, however, to draw conclusions from the story, which add general order of meaning in life; the meaning is "trapped" in the story. At this stage, God is an old man with white hair and beard. And that God takes account of intentions and enforces reciprocal justice. God's actions are like those of the child's parents. Symbols are taken as one-dimensional, and literal in meaning. In this stage the person begins to take for him/her self the stories, beliefs, and observances that symbolize belonging to his/her community. Beliefs are appropriated with literal interpretations, as are moral rules and attitudes.

There are two dangers of this stage. The first is a "works righteousness" mentality. The person at this stage thinks God is bound by the limitations of literalness, and relies on the principle of reciprocity, which can result an over-controlling, stilted perfectionism. The second danger is that the child in this stage may embrace an abasing sense of badness because of mistreatment, neglect, or the apparent disfavor of significant others.

A factor initiating transition to Stage Three is the implicit clash or contradictions in stories that leads to reflection on meanings. Santa Claus, the Easter Bunny, and the Tooth Fairy are all exposed as mythical, which leads people in this stage to begin to question the authenticity of other things they have been told.

Stage Three: Synthetic-Conventional Faith (Adolescence to Adult)

Stage Three typically has its rise and ascendancy in adolescence, but for many adults it becomes a permanent place of equilibrium. The emergent capacity of this stage is the incorporating of our past and anticipated future in an image of our own identity and faith.

The adolescent needs mirrors, literal and figurative, to keep tabs on this week's growth. He or she also needs the eyes and ears of a few trusted significant others in which to see the image of personality emerging—authority is located externally of the self. This is a "conformist" stage in the sense that it is acutely tuned to the expectations and judgments of significant others, and as yet does not have a sure enough grasp on its own identity and autonomous judgments to construct and maintain an independent perspective. When God is a significant other, the commitment to God and the correlated self-image can exert a powerful ordering on a youth's identity and values outlook. God at this stage is a companion, a guide, and a supporter.

A Stage Three person has an ideology, a more or less consistent clustering of values and beliefs, but he/she has not objectified it for examination and, in a sense, is unaware of having it. While beliefs and values are deeply felt, they typically are tacitly held—there has not been occasion to step outside them to reflect on or examine them. Differences of outlook with others are experienced as differences in this or that "kind of person."

A person's experience of the world now extends beyond the family. A number of spheres demand attention: family, school or work, peers, street society and media, and perhaps religion. Faith must synthesize values and information—it must provide a basis for identity and outlook. Symbols at this stage are not separable from what they symbolize. Demythologization feels like a fundamental threat to meaning, because meaning and symbol are bound up together. **Most of our churches work out of Stage Three Faith**.

The dangers in this stage are twofold. The expectations and evaluations of others can be so compellingly internalized that later autonomy of judgment and action can be jeopardized. Second, interpersonal betrayals can give rise either to nihilistic despair about a personal principle of ultimate being or to a compensatory intimacy with God unrelated to mundane relations.

Factors contributing to the breakdown of Stage Three and readiness for transition to Stage Four may include: serious clashes or contradictions between valued authority sources, changes by officially sanctioned leaders, or policies or practice. Previously deemed sacred and unbreachable (for example, in the Catholic church changing the mass from Latin to the vernacular, or no longer requiring abstinence from meat on Friday); the encounter with experience or perspectives that lead to critical reflection on how our beliefs and values have formed and changed, and on how "relative" they are to our particular group or background. Frequently the experience of leaving home—emotionally or physically, or both—precipitates the kind of examination of self, background, and life-guiding values that gives rise to stage transition at this point.

Stage Four: Individuative-Reflective Faith (Young Adulthood)

The self at this stage claims an identity no longer defined by the composite of our roles or meanings to others. While others and their judgments will remain important, their expectations, advice, and counsel will now be submitted to an internal panel of experts, who reserve the right to choose and who are prepared to take responsibility for their choices: the executive ego. Stage Four most appropriately takes form in young adulthood (but let us remember that many adults do not construct it, and that for a significant group, it emerges only in the mid-30s or 40s). This stage often occurs when we leave home emotionally and geographically. We look at ourselves from the outside, and are forced to examine our identity and our values.

Where genuine movement toward Stage Four is underway, we must face certain unavoidable tensions: individuality vs. being defined by a group; subjectivity and the power of our strongly felt but unexamined feelings vs. objectivity and the requirement of critical reflection; self-fulfillment or self-actualization as a primary concern vs. service to and being for others; the question of being committed to the relative vs. struggle with the possibility of an absolute.

Stage Four is a demythologizing stage, where symbols are translated into conceptual meanings. People in this stage tend to think in terms of impersonal imperatives of law, rules, and the standards that govern social rules. Stories, symbols, myths, and paradoxes from our own or other traditions may insist on breaking in upon the neatness of our previous faith.

Stage Four's dangers come from an excessive confidence in the conscious mind and critical thought and in a kind of second narcissism.

Stage Five: Conjunctive Faith (Mid-Life)

The 5th Stage moves beyond the logic of Stage Four's "either/or." It sees both sides of an issue simultaneously. Conjunctive faith goes beyond the explicit system and boundaries of identity that Stage Four worked so hard to construct.

Unusual before mid-life, this stage knows the sacrament of defeat and the reality of irrevocable commitments and acts. What the previous stage struggled to clarify, in terms of the boundaries of self and outlook, this stage now makes porous and permeable. And with the seriousness that can arise when life is more than half over, this stage is ready to spend and be spent for the cause of conserving and cultivating the possibility of others' generating identity and meaning. Ready for closeness to that which is different and threatening to self and outlook (including new depths of experience in spirituality and religious revelation), it generates and maintains vulnerability to the strange truths of those who are "other." Importantly, this involves a critical recognition of our social unconscious—the myths, ideal images, and prejudices built deeply into the self-system by virtue of our nurture within a particular social class, religious tradition, or ethnic group.

Stage Five knows that the symbols, stories, doctrines, and liturgies offered by its own and other traditions are inevitably partial, limited to a particular people's experience of God and therefore incomplete. People in this stage possess a deep knowledge of self in relation to God. They can see what Martin Buber described as the "I-thou" relationship.

The danger of this stage lies in the direction of a paralyzing passivity or inaction, giving rise to complacency or cynical withdrawal, due to its paradoxical understanding of truth.

Though Stage Five sees the divisions of the human family vividly because of the awareness of the potentially inclusive community, it remains divided. It lives and acts between an untransformed world and a transforming vision and loyalties. In some few cases this division yields to the call of the radical actualization that Fowler calls Stage Six.

Stage Six: Universalizing Faith

Stage Six is extremely rare. Stage Six becomes a disciplined, activist incarnation—a making real and tangible—of the imperatives of absolute love and justice, of which Stage Five has partial apprehensions.

Persons in Stage Six create zones of liberation from the social, political, economic, and ideological shackles we place on humanity. These universalizers are often experienced by others as subversive of the structures by which we sustain our individual and corporate survival, security, and significance. Many persons at this stage die at the hands of those whom they hope to change. They are heedlessness to self-preservation, and the vividness of their taste and feel for transcendent and religious actuality give their actions and words an extraordinary and often unpredictable quality. Life is both loved and held to loosely. They end up being more honored and revered after death than during their lives.

The rare person described by this stage has a special grace that makes them seem more lucid, more simple, and yet somehow more fully human than the rest of us. Their community is universal in extent. They generate faith compositions in which their felt sense of an ultimate environment is inclusive of all being.

Persons in Stage Six are drawn into those patterns of commitment and leadership by the providence of God and the exigencies of history. Such persons are ready for fellowship with persons at any of the other stages and from any other faith tradition.[9]

Christian Nurture in Normal Stages of Human Development

The following chart, adapted from one published by Graded Press, provides a brief overview on some major periods of human development and will help the lay pastoral caregiver get a good idea of what is typically happening in another lay person's life, and may enable them to better understand issues or concerns that are being raised.

	Main Developmental Tasks	Radius of Significant Personal Relationships	Major Problems Likely to Arise	Religious Significance of this Period	Primary Needs
Babyhood: Infants	Growing, muscle coordination, discovering limitations, and being to vocalize	The mothering person	during birth, feeding, and frustrations in the environment.	Personality being structured through experiences with significant persons. Crucial decisions are being made between basic trust and mistrust.	To be loved, fed, kept warm and dry, protected from falls, to be responded to, played with, and to experience the satisfying dependability of the mothering person.
Babyhood: Toddlers	growing, mastering of muscle use, walking, and the beginning of speech	parental persons.	societal taboos regarding the body, eating solid food, weaning from the mother's milk, and establishing a sleep schedule.	developing attitudes regarding sharing and being deprived of significant persons. The crucial decision here is between a sense of autonomy and feeling of shame and doubt of self.	permissiveness to grow at his or her own natural rate, the freedom to exercise and to explore within safe limits, protect from harmful things, to have secure and dependable relationships with parental persons and to have their affection needs satisfied.
Early Childhood: Two's	growing along with mastering more muscle skills from running and climbing. At this stage they also begin to use language in earnest.	parental persons	confinement to restricted areas, toilet training and a premature demand for moral control.	a consolidation of attitudes in regard to the body, to exploration to the world and to law and order.	understanding toilet training, freedom within secure limits, planned and supervised experiences of exploration and help in accepting temporary deprivation of parents.

	Main Developmental Tasks	Radius of Significant Personal Relationships	Major Problems Likely to Arise	Religious Significance of this Period	Primary Needs
Early Childhood: Three's and Four's	growing, exploring the widening world, mastering fine motor skills, developing social skills and mastering conversational skills.	personal relationships moves outward a little from just parents to the basic family structure.	exploration of their bodies and gender differentiation, experiencing illness, sibling rivalry, leaving home and learning what fits and belongs	centered around a consolidation of basic attitudes plus those toward birth, death and mystery. At this age the child is introduced to the larger religious group and becomes acquainted with some of the symbols of religion. This is also the time when creation and nature become important.	things like freedom and space with well defined limits, a rich variety of manipulative materials for play, opportunities for large muscle activities, contact with a number of adults, the experience of success, play time with other children, and an opportunity to explore and express feelings.
Kindergarteners	growing, playing, and talking	the basic family	during encounters with increasing moral strictures, enlarging ventures away from home, a premature demand for the mastery of symbols and concepts, and a struggle to understand, control, cause and effect relationships. Finally, it is at this stage that we confront the Oedipus-Electra situation	The religious significance of this period of life is the exploration of relationships, attitudes toward formal and organized religion, ethics of expediency and learning group moral codes, learning to express feelings, a readiness to learn and to enter into new experiences, a quest for the answers to "why?", and awareness of and response to God and an awareness of religious customs and ceremonies.	secure base of relationship in basic family from which to explore other relationships, a rich variety of experiences with things and people, freedom to play, manipulate and ask questions, opportunities for group experiences, acceptance and reassurance and protection and guidance.

	Main Developmental Tasks	Radius of Significant Personal Relationships	Major Problems Likely to Arise	Religious Significance of this Period	Primary Needs
Elementary School: First and Second Graders	developing large muscle skills, socializing in the larger world of school and acquiring the discipline of group work and play.	personal relationships expands beyond the family to people in the neighborhood and school	making adjustments to peer groups, sibling rivalry, making adjustments to authority, and identification with gender.	further development of one's own sense of values, thinking about a field of relationships, including divine, human and natural and finding satisfying meanings and relationships which give them support.	space and equipment for large muscle activity, opportunity for noise and dirt, excursions into the world, enlarging the sphere of independence, responsibility to identify with playmates of one's own gender, to achieve success, to have help in acquiring tool skills and support and assurance in failure.
Elementary School: Third and Fourth Graders	acquiring tool skills of communication by reading and writing, continuing the development of large muscle skills and socialization.	expands now to include their peer group	the demand for social conformity, winning status in peer groups, the discovery of parental fallibility and conflicts with adult standards	development of autonomous ethical values, seeing the significance of religious ideas to personal needs and activity and the beginning of the ability to understand historical relationships and their significance for Christianity.	opportunities for satisfying, self-directed work, freedom to explore more of the larger world, assistance in developing more tool skills, time and opportunities to develop peer group associations and experience in responding constructively to success and failure

	Main Developmental Tasks	Radius of Significant Personal Relationships	Major Problems Likely to Arise	Religious Significance of this Period	Primary Needs
5th and 6th Graders	social identification and perfecting the skills for communication and relating to a group.	peer group continue to grow in importance	winning social status in groups, relating warmly to friends, encountering a social caste, overcoming a fear of failure, coming to terms with authority and coping with emerging adolescent characteristics.	possibility of encouraging full ego development in human community and of developing a positive attitude toward self-controlled moral behavior through knowledge of God. It also includes the development of considerable verbal skills relating to religious thought, questioning, evaluating, forming convictions and finding identification with the people of God.	finding adequate adult and peer groups to which to relate, additional training in tool skills, help in understanding and abiding by the rules, widening contact with the world, unstructured time and space for testing oneself and challenging of one's ideas
Youth: Early Adolescence	centered on the many pubescent changes that are occurring. The adolescent is concerned about achieving social status and finding some kind of persona; significance. During this stage there is an attempt to assimilate culture and heritage as the adolescent struggles to define him or her self.	peer groups	accepting oneself as to gender, the implications of sexuality, finding a secure place in a group and beginning to move away from parents	achieving self-awareness and self-acceptance, committing oneself to the values of Christian community, structuring of a rational conscience and probing and testing the reality of adult claims	help in understanding and accepting pubescent changes, the protection of health, a wide experience in world culture, help in understanding and accepting capacities and limits, adequate images and adult guarantors.

	Main Developmental Tasks	Radius of Significant Personal Relationships	Major Problems Likely to Arise	Religious Significance of this Period	Primary Needs
Youth: Middle Adolescence	the patterning of sexual relationships.	peer group still, but also other leader who can serve as role models	making major life choices such as vocation, home and marriage, philosophy of life, citizenship, and meeting new responsibilities.	possibility of growing identification with the religious community, of accepting responsibility for moral and ethical decisions, finding leadership roles and creating the capacity of self limitations.	help in preparing to make major decisions, freedom to experiment in independence and responsibility under mature guidance, rich social experiences, and help in thinking things through
Youth: Late Adolescence	establishing a durable pattern of intimacy and vocational training	leadership models and peer groups	moving toward a final decision regarding vocation, home, marriage, a philosophy for life, citizenship and meeting new responsibilities	the increasing responsibility for participation in Christian community.	achievement of selfhood, independence, values personal identifications and finding areas of personal contribution to serve others
Adult: Young Adult	establishing a home, family, career, social status, and role in life.	spouse, children, Christian community, employer, colleagues, neighbors, parents, and in-laws.	securing and succeeding in a job, achieving an adult role, succeeding in marriage, meeting the demands of parenthood, and accepting social responsibilities	full implication of Christian ethics in decisions, has a leadership role in the Christian community, a deeper experience of Christian living, and the responsibility of the establishment of a Christian home.	getting help in problem areas, undergirding life with a Christian frame of reference and a Christian community, spiritual guidance, and help in seeing wider relationships in life

	Main Developmental Tasks	Radius of Significant Personal Relationships	Major Problems Likely to Arise	Religious Significance of this Period	Primary Needs
Adult: Middle Adulthood	carrying responsibilities for others, and finding deeper meaning and satisfaction in life.	one's spouse, children, church work associates neighbors and relatives	facing the dead ends, adjusting activity to less energy, making a living, making hard ethical choices, realizing the possibilities for continuing growth and helping grown children move toward independence.	modification of goals and discovery of more durable values within Christianity, making ethical choices, self-giving, increased opportunities for responsible leadership, a stewardship of resources and an investment in the oncoming generation	Christian fellowship, help in meeting dead ends and finding new avenues of growth, help in difficult decisions and challenging opportunities for service
Adult: Mature Adult	achieving mature satisfactions, simplifying life, maintaining a sense of worth and significance and finding meaning.	Christian community, friends, neighbors, children and grandchildren, societies and service groups.	adjusting to the changes that come with aging, finding new relationships with adult sons, daughters, and in-laws, accepting the many role and status changes that come post retirement, and coming to terms with losses.	possibility of full spiritual development and wider identification through the discovery of enduring ultimate values, opportunities for ministry to others, and finding new ways to be useful.	help in facing losses, finding compensations, and discovering meaning in the aging process, opportunities to make a continuing contribution to the community

Additional Resources

The Seasons of a Man's Life, by Daniel Levinson

Passages: Predictable Crises of Adult Life, by Gail Sheehy

Human Development Across the Lifespan, by John S. Dacey, John F. Travers and Lisa B. Fiore

Human Development, by Diane E, Papalia and Ruth Duskin Feldman

Understanding Men's Passages: Discovering the New Map of Men's Lives, by Gail Sheehy (Ballantine Books, 1999)

In a Different Voice: Psychological Theory and Women's Development, by Carol Gilligan (Harvard University Press, 1993)

Development and Faith: Where Mind, Heart and Soul Work Together, by Katherine Marshall and Marisa Bronwyn Van Saanen

Human Development and Faith: Life Cycle Stages of Body, Mind and Soul, by Felicity B. Kelcourse

Faith Development and Pastoral Care, by James W. Fowler

Becoming Adult, Becoming Christian: Adult Development and Christian Faith, by James W. Fowler

Chapter Five Review

1. Review the eight stages of ego development.
2. Try to identify episodes in your life or in the lives of others you know that are examples of how we struggle to move through the stage they have been assigned.
3. What are the results of someone not being able to move from one stage to the next, someone who is stuck in a particular stage?
4. How can this information help a lay pastoral caregiver better understand the people to whom they are assigned?
5. What is the difference between a developmental stage as defined by Erikson and the "marker events" that occur in our lives?
6. What are the periods Gail Sheehy presents in her book?
7. Reflect on your own life. What crises caused growth? Which passages identified by Sheehy have you experienced?

8. As you think about the different stages of faith, can you identify these developments in your own life? Take time to summarize each of the stages of faith.

9. How do you identify the faith journey? How might you connect Fowler's theory of faith development with the passages identified by Sheehy?

10. Review each Christian Nurture stage and the five comments that are made about them. How do these connect with your own experience? Think of other examples that relate to each stage.

11. How might you find this information helpful as you begin to work as lay pastoral caregivers?

PART III

Situations and Conditions

CHAPTER SIX

Ministry to the Whole Family Includes Children, Too

When you provide pastoral ministry, do not overlook the needs of the children and youth of the congregation. Most of what I have presented thus far can relate to them, but in this chapter I would like to center in on some of the unique needs of those who are young.

For some expert advice, I will draw upon the work of the Rita B. Hays, D. Min. Rev. Hays has served as a pastor for children for more than twenty years in a variety of settings and has taught Christian education classes on the college level. Her book, *The Children's Minister,* is inspirational and insightful.

Dr. Hays says in the introduction to her work "Children have been overlooked because of our failure to realize they, too, need a pastor. Children yearn to be recognized as persons of worth. They want pastors to know them individually and be aware of what is happening in their-lives."[10] She continues "We bless children when we focus our attention on them, offering the presence of Christ. We teach a powerful lesson to our congregations when we give children a place of priority in our busy schedules. We let others know that 'the least of these' are worthy of out love, care, and time."[11]

From that introduction Dr. Hays points out a variety of ways clergy or lay pastoral caregivers could and should be involved in the lives of children and youth. She begins by suggesting a program call Adopt-a-Grandparent. Children and youth of the congregation are paired up with older adults and amazing things happen. Relationships are built. Dividing walls crumble. Advice is shared and information relayed. Attachments are formed and an entire congregation has a better appreciation for one another. The program varies, of course, but the ones I have known usually ask older adults to sign up to serve as a mentor for a child or youth for one year. In many cases, when it is time to pair up the children and youth with older adults the next year, the people who had been together the previous ask to be reassigned to each other.

By far, the biggest advantage to this kind of program is that the older adults are not sitting in judgment of the children. They are not responsible for child rearing. They are simply there to talk, to listen, and to love the younger person. For the young person, whose own grandparents may still be working or live many miles away, this is a great opportunity to learn about things that happened fifty years ago that may influence what we do today. These people can send each other cards for birthdays and other special events. They can get together for regularly set occasions such as meals, or just ice cream. There is no limit on what might work as a reason to simply get together.

Lay pastoral caregivers could function in a similar way. If a young person needs to talk to someone or is having difficulty communicating with their parents, a lay pastoral caregiver may be just what is necessary to help that person feel loved by God and the church. Often times it is the child who is a loner or shy that feels unwelcome in youth groups and Sunday School classes. These young people may benefit from a lay pastoral caregiver who pays attention to them and listens to their concerns.

A program that could be a good follow-up to the Adopt-a-Grandparent program is one where children and young people are visited during the summer vacation from school. In this program, she suggests that the caregivers get a list of the names and address of all the children and youth in the church and devise a plan to visit each of them during the summer months. In some cases one could meet them at the pool, or invite all the children on one street to come to a "host" house for a pool party or cook out.

I concur that visiting children is very important. On one such visit to a mother and child who had requested baptism, the four-year-old girl I was going to baptize looked at me after a few minutes of conversation and said, "Say, I know who you are now. You are the man who wears that black dress!" After much laughter, I confirmed that indeed, the only times she saw me was when I was wearing my liturgical robe.

Dr. Hays includes suggestions for visitation with children. The point of the visit is to get to know the children and youth. To that end it is wise not to let the parents dominate the conversation. Pointed questions that require more than a yes or no answer will help get conversation started. Dr. Haye recommended that those who visit try to gather information regarding special interests, hobbies, and talents the young people might have. This information will be valuable in the event of a crisis in the future. Many times people find a special connection through a similar interest or ability.

One of the first kinds of crises a child will face is the death of a pet. Children develop a special attachment to their pets. Often times, these pets provide unconditional love to children. When one dies, the children experience grief. They ask questions about a dog heaven. This loss and how it is handled is a precursor for how they may handle the loss of grandparents in the future. The role of the lay pastoral caregiver is to visit, to listen to their concerns, and to answer questions as clearly as possible. Often, children will blame themselves for the death of their pet. Reassurance that death is a normal part of life will bring great comfort to the child during this crisis and for the many other deaths they will experience as they grow older. Dr. Hays developed a Service of Remembrance for a Pet that serves as a pet funeral of sorts and may assist those who are in such grief.

Other kinds of crisis that children and youth face are things like becoming a brother or sister, moving to a new city, or learning that your parents are going to divorce. All three of these situations are difficult. All of us feel alone when we are faced with the uncertainties that a crisis brings. This is especially true for children because they have not had the depth of life's experiences to assure them of God's love and of the support of others. Children are egocentric, so at times of crisis they often blame themselves and feel guilty. Lay pastoral caregivers can help children understand that there is no need for these feelings and that the adults in their lives will continue to be there to support them as they grieve.

On occasion, an accident does occur where it is the child's fault. At this point, the lay pastoral caregiver should be sure to help the family extend forgiveness and to help the adults understand what the children are experiencing.

In the situations such as a new baby or a move or a divorce, a variety of feelings may be present. Sometimes they are voiced and sometimes they are not. Knowing that these can be stressful times, it may be appropriate for a lay pastoral caregiver to pay a visit and simply ask the question, "How do you feel about . . . ?" It may be one thing to prepare for the birth of a new child, but when it comes home and gets all the attention, or shares your room, feelings may change. Children may wonder why it was necessary to have another child. They may feel less loved.

In the case of a move, guilt seldom is involved, but anger may be and fear will certainly be an emotion that is present. Talking with young people about both of these feelings will enable them to express themselves to someone and this expression is always more healthy than keeping these feelings inside. Assuring the young person that there will be new friends and a new church to welcome them may be helpful, but it is best not to discount the feelings the children have.

When parents get a divorce, everyone in the family feels a loss. For most children, the family is the center of their world. When that family is divided, the children are in a crisis. They want more than anything to have stability once again. Many questions will arise, and the uncertainty of what will happen to them keeps children unnerved and upset until these questions are answered. Very young children do not possess the ability to understand what separation means. They need stability but also need frequent but brief visits from the parent with whom they are not living. Children ages three to five must have concrete answers to their questions about divorce. They will want to know what will happen to them. They need reassured that the divorce is not their fault. Those who are ages six to eight have the ability to understand what divorce means. They may fear being abandoned and struggle with their love for both parents. The nine- to twelve-year-old child has a developed sense of right and wrong. They tend to be rigid in their beliefs. They may believe that divorce is wrong and blame both parents.

Dr. Hays tells us that in times of stress or loss children may experience symptoms of stress and anxiety, such as restlessness, loss of appetite, increased pulse, diarrhea, sleep difficulty, bad dreams, and many more.

It is not easy for young people to deal with crisis. They have had very little experience with them. By listening and offering reassurance, the lay pastoral caregiver will help the young person get through these difficult situations.

Perhaps the most difficult crisis to confront a young person is the death of someone important to them. Unfortunately, not everyone goes through the same steps at the same time. Each child will grieve in his or her own way. Again, children of different ages will understand death in different ways. The younger children may see death as temporary and seem to be not affected much by the loss. Older children may act out aggressively. Their lives have been disrupted. They need order and routine as quickly as possible. Often times children have many questions right away. After they are answered, they seem to be all right. Other children may not ask right away, but come back later and ask about the things that are on their mind. It is always best to explain briefly and simply and to answer only what you are asked. Between the ages of six and nine, children will begin to understand that death is final and permanent. At this point they may become afraid of their own death. They suddenly realize that they too will die, and it can be frightening. This age group will often blame themselves for the death if they thought unkind thoughts or said something unkind.

When children move toward the age of eleven, they will begin to develop the ability to think abstractly. They will understand that death is inevitable and irreversible.

They will begin to understand things about the body and the funeral. They will ask questions about life after death and expect straight answers.

Children have the ability to grieve intermittently. They may be upset at the funeral home, but then meet their cousins and want to go somewhere to play. This may seem strange, but perhaps this behavior protects the children from grieving too deeply.

Holidays and special occasions will be difficult for the children just like they are for adults when a loved one dies. This seems like an especially good time for a visit or a card to a child who has lost a parent or sibling.

One final area needs to be addressed regarding children and youth. This is the area of abuse. Unfortunately, far too many children are abused physically, sexually and emotionally by parents, siblings, boyfriends, girlfriends, and other people both known and unknown to them. The problem has gotten so bad that there is now a program called "Safe Sanctuaries" as a means to address it. This resource is offered as a guide or model for churches to help them create a plan for child abuse prevention. The material begins by talking about how serious the problem is and presenting facts and information, including possible signs of abuse that you might notice that would point to one kind of abuse or another. It goes on to talk about recruiting and hiring workers in a church and how important reference checks, interviews, and screenings can be before someone who works with children can be hired. One of the significant recommendations of this program is that two adults be present at all times during a church sponsored event. Abusers use secrecy, isolation, and their ability to frighten to manipulate their victims. By having two adults present, the chances of that happening are greatly reduced. The program proposes the development of a congregational plan for responding to sexual abuse.[12] If the church where the lay pastoral caregiver is a member does not participate in this program, it would be wise to get a copy of the material to review it. It would also be important for the sake of the lay pastoral caregiver and the child they are assigned to visit to make sure these visits are done in the presence of at least one other adult.

Ministry to children is a special ministry. All lay pastoral caregivers should be involved in it in some capacity. Children and youth are often overlooked when it comes to pastoral care. It would be wise to include them in any visit to a home and to make special visits just to see them as much as possible. The rewards from this special ministry are amazing.[13]

Additional Resources

Dinosaurs Divorce: A Guide for Changing Families, by Lawarence Brown and March Brown

My Parents Divorced, Too, by Maxine Ford, S. Ford and J.B. Ford

Ten keys to Successful Co-Parenting, by Melinda Blau

My Grandfather Died, by, Bernice Hogan

How It Feels When a Parent Dies, by Jill Krementz

Explaining Death to Children, by Earl A. Grollman

Chapter Six Review

1. Why is it important to minister the children and youth?
2. What are some of the changes that occur in the lives of children and youth and how the lay pastoral caregiver may be supportive during this time?
3. Have you had a personnel experience with divorce or death as a child and what do you remember about your feelings from that time?
4. How could your church begin an Adopt-A-Grandparent program and how might the lay pastoral caregivers be a part of it?
5. Several kinds of crisis have been identified regarding children. Can you envision other kinds of crisis and discuss how a child or adolescent might be able to handle it or have particular difficulty with it?

Dealing with a Crisis

There will be times when lay pastoral caregivers will be assigned to assist in a crisis situation. Every crisis is unique and no amount of training will prepare the lay pastoral caregiver for them all, but some advice from Eugene Kennedy and his book *Crisis Counseling* will be helpful.

Kennedy writes: "crisis situations are episodes in the life-span of individuals, families, groups, communities, and nations. Usually they are initiated by a hazardous event, which may be a blow from the outside or something that arises because of less bounded internal pressures. There may be one catastrophic event or a series of mishaps that have a cumulative effect."[14] It is not difficult to identify many things that can create a crisis in our lives. A sudden illness or death seems to top the list, but there are other thing that are less severe. Repeated mistakes on the job could put our jobs and livelihood in jeopardy.

In a crisis, Kennedy tells us that "the basic human balance is disturbed and the individual is rendered vulnerable."[15] New methods must be employed to regain a balance. Assistance from others may be necessary. This is where it is important to involve the lay pastoral caregiver. They can help the person get their lives back together by being there for them as quickly as possible after a crisis.

If there is no resolution, Kennedy tells us "the tension builds to a peak, then a precipitating factor can bring about the instant of crisis in which the balance is lost and the person suffers disorganization. This is the state of active crisis."[16] Active crisis is a crisis happening now. It is not passive. It is happening to someone at that very moment and it needs attention.

The person having a crisis may perceive it "1. as a threat to basic needs and independence; 2. as a loss of self-identity or some ability: or 3. as a challenge to survival, development, or mastery."

It follows that these perceptions will draw out of the person a characteristic emotional reaction.[17] That reaction can be rage, anger, crying, acts of revenge, or even suicide.

Psychiatrist Gerald Caplan, in his book, *Principles of Preventive Psychiatry*, says that we are always in situations in which we are facing problem solving actions. Normally, the tension that we feel is reduced by solving the problem we face using familiar skills. The crisis occurs when the normal problem solving actions are ineffective.

Caplan points out four characteristic phases in the development of a crisis. They are:

1. The problem causes tension that mobilizes the person's habitual problem-solving responses.
2. The failure of these responses, and the continuing unmet need, produce inner disturbances such as anxiety, guilt, and disorganization of functioning.
3. When the tension passes a certain point, it becomes a powerful stimulus to the mobilization of additional crisis-meeting resources such as exploring by trial and error either thoughts or actions not previously taken.
4. If the tension is not resolved, the tension of the unmet need mounts until it reaches another threshold; which is the breaking point where mental illness occurs.

Caplan also identifies two kinds of crises: developmental and accidental. The developmental crises are "normal" in the sense that they happen as an integral part of growth. Examples might be birth, weaning, toilet training, going to school, and so forth. Accidental crises are precipitated by an abnormal and often unexpected loss of what we might feel is an essential source of need satisfaction. These could be things like a loss of a job, money, a very close support person, status, an incapacitating accident or illness, etc.[18]

We face both kind of crises and handle them as best we can. The church and the lay pastoral caregiver who represents the church can be supportive and helpful during this time of crises.

It is not the job of the lay pastoral caregiver to be the pastoral counselor, but they can serve as a good sounding board for the person in crises as they try to talk through what they are thinking or feeling at the moment. For those people who do not "talk their think," it may be more difficult to be helpful except for what has been commonly called a "ministry of presence." In this case, just being there for the person during their crises can be comforting for them. Here is where the good listening skills will be helpful. The lay pastoral caregiver needs to pay very close attention to the few words that are being said as well as the non-verbal communication coming from the person in crises. Prayer will also be important. Lift the person up in prayer and give him or her hope that in the midst of this crisis, as bad as it may seem, God will be with him or her to see things through.

Like Caplan, Eugene Kennedy identifies three kinds of crises: In the first instance we find someone who has been functioning for a long time in emergency conditions. In this case, there may be lots of stress, but the person is holding up pretty well. The crisis occurs when the person reaches the point of exhaustion and is no longer able to cope. This is a good example of burn-out. They person simply comes to a point when they can no longer function appropriately. These people need to step away from the situation and rest for a while. A person who is caring for an ill loved one day after day can get to this point. The church can help by providing respite care programs to give these folks a brief break.

The second type of crises arises when there is some unexpected change. A good example there is the death of a loved one, or the loss of a job, or a stock market crash that triggers an overwhelming release of emotion. This is one of the most common kinds of crises. It is temporary and reversible with time.

The third kind of crises is one where the person actually originates their own crises. Some people work better under pressure and tend to place undo pressure upon themselves.[19]

It requires a listening attitude, a willingness to suspend judgment and the ability to put oneself in the other person's shoes to be effective at assisting others through a crisis. Actively listening to what is being said through words, body language, and inflection will enable the lay pastoral caregiver to better understand the issue. In a crisis, there is no time to waste in repeating what is on one's mind. It is important that the lay pastoral caregiver begin by listening intently. While listening, it is also important to remain open and not jump to conclusions. In a crisis, the person needs people around him or her who will keep an open mind, who are not there to judge, but are there to support. By imagining him- or herself in the position of the person in crisis, the lay pastoral caregiver may develop a better understanding of what it must be like in this particular situation. Then, perhaps they can be of assistance.

One of the tools employed by pastoral counseling is to listen until the person being counseled is able to articulate the concerns they have. A second is to help the person focus on possible solutions by asking appropriate questions. The typical "How does that make you feel?" gets to the depth of emotions, but in the case of a crisis, the purpose of the questions need to be for providing clarity so that the person begins to see the issue clearly and is able to take appropriate steps to work through the crisis. It is important for the lay pastoral caregiver to be themselves, to respond naturally. They are not sent to give advice or tell people what to do. They can however, ask questions that require the person in crisis to think, to respond, to begin to move toward making decisions and putting one foot in front of the next on the path toward recovery.

An example of how this might work is in a situation involving a death. Let us assume that a teenager has been killed in an accident. The lay pastoral caregiver needs to listen to the words and cries of the parents and siblings as they mourn the loss of this child. The caregiver can imagine what it must be like to lose a teenage child, full of promise and with a full life ahead. To help this family, the lay pastoral caregiver can ask about funeral arrangements, if family members have been notified, and if the family would like to use the church for a family meal after the funeral. By helping the family focus on the next step and the one after that, the lay pastoral caregiver will enable the family to move through the crises a little bit at a time until they are able to cope on their own once again.

This is an example of how that scene might occur:

"Hello, I'm Mr. Smith. Rev. Jones asked me to stop by to see if I can be of assistance. May I come in?"

"Yes. I'm sorry, what was your name again? I know I've seen you at church, but I haven't been very active."

"I'm John Smith. I'm one of the lay pastoral caregivers from the church. Rev. Jones has told me about the accident and I just wanted to come by express my sympathy and to see if I could be of assistance."

"Thank you. Please have a seat. Honey, Mr. Jones is here from the church. Could you come here?"

"Hello Mrs. Smith. I'm John Jones. I'm a lay pastoral caregiver from the church. I'm here to support you in any way I can."

"Thank you. Rev. Jones said someone would come by. Tell me, have you ever had a son die?"

"No, I have not. It must be terrible to have to go through this."

"You're right about that. Our son was just seventeen. He was supposed to graduate next week. Some drunk took his life away. He had it all. He was smart, good looking, popular. Now he is gone. Oh, dear God! He's gone!"

"I remember your son from when he was in the youth choir. My son is about three years older than he was. I know this is a very difficult time for you and I am here to help in any way I can."

"Can you bring back our son?"

"No. I'm afraid I cannot, nobody can do that, but perhaps I can help you get through the next few days. Tell me, have you made arrangements with a funeral home yet?"

"We have selected one, but have not talked to anyone yet. We have an appointment for this afternoon."

"I remember when my father died that there were some hard decisions that we had to make at that first meeting with the funeral director. They will want obituary information, and you will need to choose a casket. That was the toughest part for me. Have you selected a cemetery or do you have grave plots anywhere?"

"No. I guess we will have to find something."

"The funeral director can help you with that."

"How about the funeral service? Have you discussed that with Rev. Jones?"

"No, he just told us that he would be available anytime we decided to have the funeral."

"When the service is over, would you like the church to provide a meal in our fellowship hall for your family and guests?"

"Would they do that?"

"Sure. We have some very good cooks, and they like to serve in this way. There are many fine people in our church and we all want to help in whatever way we can."

"That would be nice."

"Mr. and Mrs. White, here is my card with my name and phone number. I will do anything I can for you. Please call me if you need anything. I will be back in touch with you tomorrow to see what arrangements you have made. Perhaps then you can tell me what time the service will be and I'll be in touch with the church members who make the meals. In the mean time, I will be praying for you both. I believe we find the strength we need at times like this through prayer."

"Thank you, Mr. Smith. We'll talk to you tomorrow."

By directing the conversation and pushing for some decisions, people are able to move a baby step at a time in a situation that might easily bog them down. By offering support, sympathy and suggestions, Mr. Smith was able to help a family in grief.

A loss does not have to be as serious as the death of a family member to be a crisis. It can be any loss. For teenagers, it might be the end of a friendship or breaking up with a boyfriend or girlfriend. For younger children it may be the death of a pet. These things can cause a crisis. Adults have been through these things already, but a job loss can cause major problems within a household. Consider the implications of loosing a job. This is what Kennedy refers to a crisis due to an unexpected change. There is the financial disaster that may occur very quickly for some families who do not have sufficient savings or family support. But just as important are the emotional feelings of failure. Depression can result if the person did something to warrant the job loss. Even if that were not the case, one still feels at fault somehow, and in need of some help in figuring out next steps. Every local church should have a list of members who are in a position of helping someone find a new job. The church can also provide assistance in writing resumes and sharpening skills. The pastor should make sure he or she knows how unemployment works and can share this information with lay pastoral caregivers who work with people who have lost their jobs. The pastor may want to ask someone who works for the unemployment commission to come to talk to the lay pastoral caregivers one evening. The more information that the church can provide to the person who has lost his or her job, the quicker they will be able to move forward in finding another. The job of the lay pastoral caregiver is to help move people through these crises by listening and making appropriate suggestions. Step by step, people make their way past the events using whatever coping mechanisms they have developed. The church can assist them and the lay pastoral caregiver can act as a guide to help them focus on how to move beyond the event and toward resolution.

Additional Resources:

Coping with Counseling Crisis: First Aide for Christian Counselors, by Jay E. Adams

Pastoral Counseling With People in Distress, by Harold J. Haas

Chapter Seven Review

1. What are the two ways Caplan defines a crisis?
2. What are the three ways Kennedy tells us a person may perceive

a crisis? How do you understand the differences between the Caplan and Kennedy definitions?

3. Review again the situation where the family is in grief over the loss of their son. What other ways could one have assisted the family during this first meeting?

CHAPTER EIGHT

Illnesses & Healing

When you consider a congregation is made up of members who range in age from birth to 100, it is obvious that not everyone has or will have the conditions listed in this chapter. However, there are some common ailments and diseases that our church members may struggle with. This information in presented in general terms and is not intended as a substitute for medical diagnosis or medical care. Those things are best left up to the physicians. The information provided here is designed to help the lay pastoral caregiver better understand medical illnesses.

Aging

There are several theories regarding why and how people age. They can be categorized into one of two general classes. The first class or group of theories are called intrinsic, or "biological clock" theories. As the name may imply, the belief here is that we are biologically programmed to age the way we do. The "programmed" theories claim that the aging process is generated intentionally by organisms within the body, by the readout of a program that is encoded within the DNA of the body's cells. Aging is seen in much the same way as the development and maturation of an individual. It is an extension of the normal developmental process, with some variation produced by interaction with one's environment. The general concept is that a biological clock is located somewhere in the body or in

the cells, which at a certain time turns on or turns off specific genes leading to age-related changes in the body. Many people place this biological
clock with the brain.

The second class of biological theories of aging are called the extrin-
sic, stochastic, or "wear and tear" theories. These theories compare our
bodies to that of a machine. The genes provide the body with a strong and
viable physiology at about the time of sexual maturity. Over time, one's
physiology degenerates due to normal unavoidable damage to body tissues, as well as abuse we heap upon ourselves. Ultimately, the accumulated damage causes failure of some critical biological system, and death
results. In this theory, aging is a passive process, produced by internal and
external agents, which cause damage to the body's systems.

There are some syndromes that have been identified that give great
validity to the "biological clock" theory. The Hutchinson-Gilford syndrome and the Werner's syndrome are examples wherein people with
these rare genetic mutations are doomed to a short life in which many of
the hallmarks of advanced age occur very early in life. Yet these cases are
rare, and perhaps the more "normal" aging occurs as our bodies simply
wear out over time.

Alexander Leaf, in a study published in *Scientific American*, compared
people who were 75 years old with persons who were 30 years old. He
found that those who were 75 years old had 92% of their former brain
weight, 84% of their former basal metabolism, 70% of their former kid-
ney filtration rate, and 43% of their former maximum breathing capacity.[20] What he is telling us with these statistics is that on average, when
people reach age 75, their brain weighs 10% less, their bodies are burn-
ing calories at a reduced rate, their kidneys are filtering about three fourth
as fast, and their lungs process oxygen more slowly. The implications of
this information are that there is a decrease or decline in the physical body
as it ages.

Though Leaf's data compares people aged 30 to those aged 75, aging
is not an event that happens suddenly. It is, as one would assume, a gradual, continuous process that begins at birth. We know that at least some

of the systems of the body decline at different rates in different individuals. They do, however, decline in all people, from the point of their fullest development to a point where they have lost much of their abilities.

A study done by doctors Robert Kane, Joseph Ouslander, and Itmar Abrass in 1989 indicates that under normal circumstances, the body rejects foreign cells, but as the body ages, there is a progressive weakening of the immune system. The result of this weakening is that the elderly become more susceptible to respiratory and other illnesses.[21] For that reason, the elderly are encouraged to get flu shots each fall and tend to be more careful about colds and traveling, even to worship, in bad weather. Younger people, who are in better physical shape, may not need these shots to fight off the flu virus.

Choosing between these two classes of theories is less important than understanding the differences and being aware that no matter how we age, the fact remains that we do so. If we are fortunate, we all get older, and as we do, our bodies change.

Cardiovascular Disease

Like the immune system, which is affected by the aging process, so too is the cardiovascular system affected. The degradation of the functional ability of the cardiovascular system usually interferes with the much-needed supply of nutrients and oxygen to the cells. As a result, the tissues and organs of the body are damaged. This damage leads eventually to the decline of other major processes.

As we age, we run a greater risk of cardiovascular diseases. Taken as a group, they are the number one cause of death in our society. These diseases include a wide range of disorders that may destroy the blood vessels of the heart. The combination of these diseases is the leading cause of death throughout the world. Such things as heredity, poor nutrition, and the environment may influence them.

The circulatory system is made up of two interconnected systems. They both begin at the heart. These systems are called the systemic circulation system and the pulmonary circulation system. In the systemic system, the blood is pumped from the left ventricle of the heart into the aorta. Then the blood moves into smaller and smaller arteries until it comes to the very small capillaries where the blood actually moves through the body tissues. After it flows through this tissue, it starts on its return trip to the heart, being collected by veins until it enters the right atrium.

The pulmonary system circulates the blood from the right ventricle into the pulmonary arteries and through the lung capillaries. It is here, in the lung capillaries, that the blood picks up the much-needed oxygen and moves by veins back to the heart through the left atrium. Since the capillaries are the areas where the oxygen and foodstuffs go into the body cells, and where waste products are removed, any vascular disease is sure to affect in some way the function of the tissues that are supplied by the capillaries.

There are two major types of cardiovascular disease: artery disease and vein disease. The most significant cause of artery disease is the thickening and hardening of the artery walls by deposits of fatty materials. These deposits may occur as a result of a fatty diet, high blood pressure, or any number of genetic factors. The second type, vein disease, involves the formation of blood clots. These clots usually form in the legs. The major factors that cause these blood clots are: 1. Slowing of the blood stream. 2. The increase of ability of the blood to coagulate, and 3.An injury to the lining of the vein. Clots that form may break off and travel to the right side of the heart. From there, the clot may be pumped to the lung, but it gets trapped, as the pulmonary artery gets smaller. Once trapped, the clot may block or restrict the flow of blood to a portion of the lung creating a pulmonary infarction. The immediate shock may be fatal. We see this kind of problem most often in postoperative hospital patients. Though it seems cruel, it is important that our parishioners who have just undergone surgery get up and walk as soon as possible to avoid the possibility of these clots forming in their legs.

Related to cardiovascular disease is heart disease. Most heart diseases are related to insufficient blood supply to the body tissues we talked about above or overwork of the heart muscle. There are two kinds of heart diseases. They are either congenital or acquired. Congenital disorders result from abnormal development of the heart, but acquired disorders are due to heredity, environment, and infectious processes that cause damage to the heart, the arteries, the valves, or the conduction tissue.

Some of the more common risk factors for coronary artery disease are: smoking, elevated cholesterol levels, obesity, hypertension, and diabetes mellitus.

People with cardiac problems usually require a strict low sodium, low cholesterol diet. Sticking to a diet can be one way to reduce the risk of a heart attack.

During visits to these parishioners, do not bring any food except for the spiritual food they so desperately need. The job of the pastor and lay pastoral caregiver is to encourage your parishioners to continue the hard work of exercise and restraint. Be aware of their limitations and do not overstay your welcome.

Cancer

In modern society, cancer is the second leading cause of death. Cancer has been known and described throughout history, although its greater prevalence today is certainly due to the conquest by medical science of most infectious diseases and to the increased life span of humans.

In the United States in the early 1990s more than one fifth of all deaths were caused by cancer. In 1993 the American Cancer Society predicted that about 33% of all Americans will eventually develop some form of the disease. Skin cancer is the most prevalent cancer in both men and women, followed by prostate cancer in men and breast cancer in women. Lung cancer, however, causes the most deaths in both men and women.

Cancer is the common term used to designate the most aggressive and usually fatal forms of a larger class of diseases known as neoplasms, which are heritably altered, relatively autonomous growths of tissue. A neoplasm is autonomous in that it does not fully obey the biological mechanisms that govern the growth and metabolism of individual cells and the overall cell interactions. The changes seen in a neoplasm are heritable in that these characteristics are passed on from one cell to its progeny, or daughter cells.

The principle classification of neoplasms as either benign or malignant relates to their behavior. Several relative differences distinguish the two classes. A benign neoplasm is encapsulated, but malignant neoplasms are not. Malignancies grow more rapidly than do benign forms, and invade adjacent, normal tissue. Tissue of a benign tumor is structured in a manner similar to that of the tissue from which it is derived; malignant tissue, however, has an abnormal and unstructured appearance.

Types of Cancer

BREAST CANCER

According to the American Cancer Society, breast cancer is the leading killer of women worldwide. The majority of cases occur in post-menopausal women. When breast cancer is diagnosed, treatment begins with surgical removal of the cancer. Most patients are then given radiation and/or chemotherapy treatments to make sure that all the cancer is destroyed. No one cause for breast cancer has been identified, but diet is believed to play a role.

Perhaps the best thing that the lay pastoral caregiver can do is to be open to listening to the fears and concerns of the women who find out that they have breast cancer. It may be good to try to put a newly diagnosed parishioner to touch with someone who has gone through a similar experience. One-on-one support and group support can be very helpful.

The woman with breast cancer is not the only person who may need counseling after a diagnosis. Husbands and adult children may also need someone to hear their fears and concerns. Issues relating to physical disfigurement and loss of intimacy are concerns that must be dealt with by spouses. Children may be sympathetic toward their mothers, but soon they will begin to become concerned about their own health and the possibility that they too may develop breast cancer. Listening ears, one-on-one support, and group support can help all involved through this very trying time after diagnoses of breast cancer.

LUNG CANCER

Lung cancer is caused primarily by smoking. Cigarette smoke contains many initiating and promoting agents, placing at risk smokers and non-smokers who are regularly exposed to secondary smoke. Genetic factors may play some role in this disease, since only about 70% of smokers develop lung cancer. By the time this cancer is diagnosed, the cancer has usually metastasized to the point where surgery, radiation, and chemotherapy are not effective.

It is difficult for some people to be supportive or sympathetic of those who have lung cancer. In most cases, those who have this kind of cancer are responsible for their condition. They are not a "victim." These church members are addicted and have never been able to get away from this addiction. However, support and not reproach is needed here as well.

PROSTATE CANCER

Prostate cancer is the second most common cancer in men. Unlike many other cancers, the incidence of prostate cancer increases dramatically with age; over 80% of all such cancers are diagnosed in men over the age of 65. Like breast cancer, early detection of prostate cancer is important. The annual rectal examination is still one of the best ways to detect prostate cancer in older men. Treatment of this disease involves surgery, radiation, and the use of hormones and chemotherapeutic drugs. The good news is that prostate cancer patients have excellent survival rates, exceeding 75%.

It would be good if the clergy could ask a man who has been one of those 75% to talk with someone who has been recently diagnosed. Those who have recovered are living proof that cancer of this type can be successfully treated. It would be good if the church office could keep track of who has had what surgery so that those who have done well could be of encouragement to those facing the same procedure. When a situation comes up where the pastor thinks another church member may be helpful, the pastor should ask them to assist in whatever way they feel comfortable. For men this is usually a sensitive issue. The lay pastoral caregivers should be sensitive people who could deal with this issue. It is best to assign the most sensitive lay pastor to the most sensitive situations.

Skin Cancer

One of the most common and preventable cancers, is usually caused by exposure to sunlight. The risk of developing skin cancer can be greatly decreased by limiting skin exposure to sunlight by wearing hats and light clothing or by using sun blocks to prevent the dangerous ultraviolet rays from damaging the skin. The most common types of skin cancer are readily diagnosed, treated, and cured at the early stages.

Other Cancer Facts

Cancer-causing agents, chemical, biological or physical, are termed carcinogens. Chemicals that cause cancer have a variety of molecular structures and include complex hydrocarbons, aromatic amines, and certain metals, drugs, hormones, and naturally occurring chemicals in molds and plants. Several drugs used to treat cancer are also carcinogenic; although these chemicals are used to break DNA strands of cancer cells, thereby killing the cancer cells, this same property causes the agent to induce cancer in normal cells.

In general, cancer is not the direct result of genetic inheritance. However, several cancers, including cancer of the colon, breast, and prostate exhibit a familial predisposition. While these types of cancer exhibit a dominant mode of inheritance, they are recessive, requiring the alteration of both copies of the affected gene in order for a cell to become malignant.

The best we can do as pastors and lay pastoral caregivers is to become knowledgeable about these various kinds of cancers and share that knowledge with our church members. Knowledge about the disease will give some comfort to person diagnosed. The pastor and lay pastoral caregiver can offer knowledgeable support and help set reasonable expectations.

Sight

As we age, we experience more difficulty with our sight. One of those difficulties is regarding adaptation to lighting levels. Adaptation to lighting levels, especially early-dark adaptation, takes longer for seniors because the lens of the eye thickens with age, causing less light to pass through. A condition, called *presbyopia*, decreases the ability for the eye to focus on close-up objects with age. The pupil diameter becomes smaller, causing less light to enter the eye. *Cataracts* cause a clouding of the lens and a decrease in the amount of light able to enter the eye. All of these normal changes to the eye as we age present a challenge.

Another visual impairment to consider is the *yellowing of the lens*. As we age, the lens of the eye not only thickens, but begins to yellow. The older we get the more difficult is becomes to discriminate among shorter wavelength colors. Reds and yellows are colors can be more easily discerned than blues and greens.

Getting around becomes more challenging as we age, and some of that is related to changes in vision. Negotiating steps (identifying stair height) and driving become difficult because of *changes in depth perception* and diminished visual acuity.

Macular degeneration is another common eye problem that afflicts people as they age. In this case, there is a loss of sight in the middle of the eye and often, the loss of sight all together is the result.

Hearing

There's a reason older people are stereotypically cast as hard of hearing. Hearing loss is the most common characteristic of aging. *Presbycusis* is a term used to describe any hearing impairment in old age; especially as it relates to high frequency tones. That is why some older people say, "I can hear him just fine," when referring to a male with a deep voice. For some, louder sounds are hard to distinguish, and consonants become harder to understand.

People who may be hard of hearing or are in the category of the "late deafened" may:

- position themselves to see the speaker's face;
- watch faces intently;
- look blank or puzzled when unable to understand;
- make inappropriate responses, or no responses;
- frequently ask the speaker to repeat; or
- have difficulty understanding with background noise.

Those who are deaf may:

- appear to be alert but fail to respond to spoken language;
- not respond to noise or other sound;
- follow every move with their eyes; or
- point to their ear or mouth, perhaps while shaking their heads.

Understanding that many elderly have some degree of hearing loss may help the lay pastoral caregiver remember to sit near and speak to the person with the hearing loss. It is important that they can see the speaker's face as they seek to understand.

Sleep

As people age, normal age-related changes occur in sleep patterns. They often find it difficult to either fall asleep or to sleep without waking several times each night. The result is that they are tired.

Sleep apnea is defined as cessation of breathing for over ten seconds at least five times in an hour. These episodes often result in an awakening and can seriously disturb sleep. As many as 25% of all adults may fit this categorization, with a larger fraction being men. The most successful treatment for sleep apnea is wearing a mask that applies positive pressure to the airway, and keeps it open.

This list offers an overview of health conditions that affect those for whom we care. While this section seems to contain a lot of information, it is only a brief summary of health conditions. I intend this information for guidance, not as medical advice and not as a set of diagnostic tools. My basic purpose is that as we engage in ministries of caring for others, learning more about these health conditions increases our understanding and compassion for our brothers and sisters.

Healing

We who are Christians believe that our God can and does lend healing. It gives us hope in the face of despair and confidence to move on after trauma. I have known for years and have witnessed for myself in my own family, in my ministry in the local church, and in my ministry to the elderly that faith can help in the healing process. We have all seen the miracles of healing when all hope was gone, but what I would like to talk about is the not so miraculous, but still significant, healing that occurs every day with our elderly church members.

An article by Malcolm McConnell on how faith can heal appeared in the October 1998 Readers Digest. In that article, Mc Connell related a study done by Dr. Harold Koenig, an associate professor of psychiatry at Duke University. As a result of studies done on thousands of American since 1984, Dr. Koenig determined that "religious faith not only promotes overall good health, but also aides in recovery from serious illness." According to Dr. Koenig, through prayer, religious patients "acquire an indirect form of control over their illness." The article indicates that those who attended worship at least once a week spent, on average, about four days in a hospital while others who did not attend as often spent ten to twelve days hospitalized. This information has been confirmed by other studies around the world that see health benefits related to post surgery recovery, heart attacks, and strokes. McConnell noted a study done at Yale University that looked at over 2,800 people over the age of 65. Those who never or seldom attended worship "had nearly twice the stroke rate" as those who attend regularly.

The physiology involved in the noted healing begins with a reduction of stress. My family practice physician told me that 75% of the patients who come to see him have a stress-related illness. Heart disease, hypertension, panic attacks, asthma, insomnia, and many more illnesses and diseases have stress as a major factor in their occurrence. We know that prayer, and especially meditation, can relieve stress. One of the things I learned as a tool to meditation was the value of repetitive prayer. It helps us center in and focus, but at the same time, it slows us down. Our heart rate decreases, our breathing slows, we relax and remain relaxed as we pray.

Dr. Koenig discovered in his studies that stress impairs the immune system. When we are stressed, our body creates an inflammatory agent called "interleukin-6," which is "associated with chronic infections, diabetes, cancer and cardiovascular disease." Koenig found high levels of interleukin-6 in the blood levels of those who seldom or never attended worship. On the other hand, those who attended worship on a regular basis had significantly lower levels of interleukin-6 in their blood. The obvious conclusion is that those who pray cope better with the stresses that confront us all.[22]

Most diseases affected by stress are diseases often associated with the elderly. Heart disease, cancer, and diabetes are common among the elderly. Perhaps the church could make an effort to impress upon those who are middle aged the importance of prayer and faith in creating good health. For the elderly who are afflicted by these diseases, the power and practice of prayer can be very beneficial.

Faith, healing, and good health go hand in hand. The last assisted living facility I directed was very much aware of the need for healing of body, mind, and spirit. We made devotions, worship, and prayer a part of our everyday lives. I was never surprised when our care plans revealed that a resident was doing better and needed less medical attention. We tried to minister to our residents in a holistic manner. I believe that central to Jesus' teachings is a concept of love that is fundamental in all our interactions with one another. It is the basis for giving care, receiving care, healing, and future hope. Jesus understood love as complete devotion to God and to one another. Experiencing God's love enables us to love others in return. This can easily be translated into caring for the elderly, the ill, and the infirmed. We assist the healing process through our love and devotion. We encourage good health through good nutrition and exercise. We enable faith to grow through devotions, worship, and one-on-one conversation. The church can do the same for its members in a wide variety of ways.

The role of the local church pastor and lay pastoral caregivers in this healing process is essential. Visits to facilities where a parishioner is living are very important. Encouragement to get well, hang in there, and do better is essential in the healing process. You would be surprised to learn how important a visit from a minister is to the older adult who is in a long-term care facility. They look forward with pride and anticipation to the day when their minister or another member of their church is to come. They share their news with those who dine with them, tidy up a little more and do their best to be prepared for the visit.

An older minister friend of mind told me that one of the things he did as a nursing home Chaplin was to make appointments with the residents before he left. He was convinced that it gave the resident something to look forward to in what can be lonely days. When he shared his philosophy with me, I was reminded of several of the shut-in members of the congregations I served who were prepared for my visit when I came to share communion. They had the coffee table covered with a white cloth, a Bible from which to read, and refreshments prepared for us to enjoy. By setting an appointment ahead of time, I could be sure that the person was going to be home, not at the doctors or on another necessary trip. Planning ahead then gives the older person something to look forward to and it ensures that the pastor does not waste time.

Nutrition

The elderly are believed by some to require fewer calories in their diet than when they were younger because of a reduction in body weight, a decrease in metabolic rate and a decline in activity. These factors do suggest a need for fewer calories, but at the same time, there is an increased demand for nutrients to help the elderly resist the effects of disease. Unfortunately, many elderly do not bother fixing a good meal for themselves, especially if they are single. They end up eating what is easy or quick and are not as concerned as they should be about the nutritional value of the food. There are many vitamin supplements available that can help the elderly person remain healthy.

One way our society has found to help the elderly stay healthy is through the variety of Meals On Wheels programs. Healthy warm meals are delivered to the residences of the recipient at noon. Most programs offer an additional sandwich for a lighter evening meal. All of the Meals On Wheels programs I have known have been church-related. A church or a group of churches prepares the meals and serves them. The meals act not only as a means of providing good, warm food, but also as a point of contact from the church to the parishioner. In many cases, this contact is the only one the elderly person may have all day.

Some churches use these meal deliveries as a means of checking to ensure that the elderly are OK. I am aware of at least two occasions in the programs with which I have related, that the alert delivery volunteer prompted police and medical attention for elderly women who and fallen and broken their hips. Because they lived alone and could not move, they were unable to get the assistance they needed.

Nutrition and healing are complementary, and good nutrition helps maintain goo health. Vitamin E is helps maintain for good eye health. Iron is an essential part of all cells, and is found in dark green leafy vegetables. Low sodium diets can help keep blood pressure in check. Low fat and low cholesterol diets assist those with cardiovascular problems. High fiber diets often are necessary for good digestion and regular bowel movements.

Diabetics can reduce their need for medication by carefully monitoring their diets. Diabetics also need to continue to consult with their primary care physicians. Nutrition remains an essential aspect of health and wellness.

In all conditions, as Christians we remember the importance of prayer. The author of 1 Thessalonians concluded that letter with words that are appropriate to conclude this chapter: Rejoice always, pray without ceasing, give thanks in all circumstances; for this is the will of God in Christ Jesus for you. (I Thessalonians 5:16-18)

Additional Resources

The Art of Getting Well: Maximizing Health and Well-being When You Have a Chronic Illness, by David Spero and Martin L. Rossman

Families Living with Chronic Illness and Disabilities : Interventions, Challenges and Opportunities, by Paul W. Power and Arthur E. Dell Orto

Chronic Illness in Children: an Evidence Based Approach, edited by Paul W. Power and Arthur E. Dell Orto

The Anatomy of Hope: How People Prevail in the Face of Illness, by Jerome Groopman

Fear Not: Learning from Your Cancer, by Judy Gattis Smith (Discipleship Resources, 2008)

Healing Power of Faith: How Belief and Prayer Can Help You Triumph Over Disease, by Harold Koenig and Malcolm McConnell

Healing Bodies and Souls: A Practical Guide for Congregations, by W. Daniel Hale and Harold G. Koenig

Healing, by Francis MacNutt

Healing Words, by Larry Dossey

Chapter Eight Review

1. Review all of the medical needs outlined in the chapter.
2. Identify the diseases that most often cause death in your community.

3. Think about the role the lay pastoral caregiver might play in helping the parishioners cope with these illnesses.
4. Imagine your own comfort level if you are assigned a parishioner who has one of these conditions.
5. What is the difference between physical and spiritual healing?
6. Have you ever known anyone who has been healed? What was your response?
7. Why are some people healed while others are not?
8. How do you feel about Dr. Koenig's findings in relation to faith and healing?

CHAPTER NINE

Suffering & Grief

Suffering

One of the many things the lay pastoral caregiver will face in ministry is suffering. People in the congregation will have terminal illnesses. As a result of a crisis, people will suffer loss. Perhaps they have been suffering from some affliction of their own. The role of the lay pastoral caregiver is to hear about the pain and in some way to provide some hope to those who suffer.

In Derrel Watkins's book, *Practical Theology for Aging*, Kellie Shantz writes "True hope must be discovered in a present that, even in its experience of suffering, is alive with possibilities. For those whose present is imbued with pain and torment, the message of hope must begin in the immediacy of the crucifixion experience. Such hope must be grounded firmly in the knowledge that in the cross of Jesus Christ, God assumed all suffering, and in the resurrection, God has overcome all suffering. Individuals can summon the strength to carry their own cross of suffering when they have the assurance that while God does not preserve us from all suffering he does preserve us in all suffering."[23]

The distinction made by Shantz is significant. Somehow we all assume that we should never suffer, never hurt, never experience pain, that if we are good Christians only good things will happen to us. But that is not life. That is not reality. The best of people suffer and die. We all die. Suffering from a disease as we age is normal. Fighting the battle against cancer or heart disease or arthritis is something many people go through before they receive the gift of eternal life. The point to be made here is that **God does not cause suffering**. It is not a punishment for sins. God, however can be there for the person as they suffer. God's presence will preserve them as they struggle with their illness, and that is the point the lay pastoral caregiver can and should make.

The important question for those who suffer is, according to Shantz, " 'How does God relate to our suffering?' The answer, and the fundamental source of hope for those who suffer, lies in the knowledge that God, out of infinite love for the created, suffers with us. The cross signifies that God never directly inflicts suffering. In the cross, God accepts the suffering that befalls God. Thus, we have a glimpse of the depth of God's love for us in the suffering of his Son on the cross. The cross is the extent to which God is willing to go to reconcile humanity to God's self. That God suffers with us and knows us fully means that we can bring our suffering to a God that knows; we do not have to explain or beseech a God who doesn't know suffering."[24]

Jesus' suffering and death was one in which he made the decision to follow the will of God, the God he called "Abba," father. It was for Jesus an act of surrender, an act of perfect obedience. The surrender was done out of love for God and love for humanity. And he suffered as he was beaten and crucified.

In Christ, we find God going out of himself to be in solidarity with the afflicted. Jesus brings the companionship of God to people who feel forsaken and abandoned. Therefore there is no amount of suffering that can ever cut us off from God.

We find in Jesus an example of one who knew he would suffer and prayed about it. There, in the garden of Gethsemane, Jesus prayed that God would find another way to work his will. It is a good example for all who suffer and for those who minister to them. Prayer is transformative. The person who prays is changed. By seeking God's help we put ourselves in a position to receive it. By praying, we are strengthened and given hope. And when we have hope, our suffering is abated and we are given a reason to struggle on. And even if in the end of our struggle, we die, for the Christian, the suffering and sacrifice made by our God gives us new life where there is no suffering, and we abide for eternity with our God.

The Grief Process

Grief is the emotional, behavioral reaction of the person who suffers a loss. Bereavement is the reconciliation or perhaps the integration of this loss in our lives. It is a process that follows grieving. The reconciliation takes place a little at a time until finally, we are able to say that we are over the grieving and have accepted the hurt that accompanies loss. Mitchell and Anderson, in their book *All Our Losses All Our Griefs* say that grief is universal, inescapable, even when its existence and impact are denied. It is a composite of powerful emotions confronting us when we lose someone or something we value. It is the work we engage in that enables us to eventually live full, satisfying lives.[25]

There are certain dynamics of grief. Grief emotions tend to be grouped into five different clusters. The first of these emotions is emptiness. This may include loneliness or isolation. When we feel empty, we feel somehow diminished from within. Loneliness is the sense that one's surroundings are also empty of any of the people who matter or care. Isolation is the sense of being defined from others by some invisible boundary. A second dynamic of grief is fear and anxiety. Prior to the anticipated death of a loved one, we may feel the dread of abandonment. Afterward, we experience the anxiety of separation. We ask ourselves, "What am I ever going to do without him/her?" The third dynamic of grief deals with guilt and shame. As you can imagine, guilt is a dominant component of grief. We feel guilty when we assume responsibility for the loss, made decisions that may have in some way hastened the loss or have not had an opportunity to resolve hurt feelings in our relationship with the person who has died. (Remember the "turtles" from chapter 4?) As church leaders you have heard these kinds of comments often. Anger is the fourth dynamic of grief. When the loss is death, the anger is often times directed at other family members, medical personnel, or God. (Remember that some people are "skunks," spraying their anger on anyone within range.) Sadness and despair are also dynamics we see often in grief. It is normal to feel sad over the loss of something. The degree of sadness is usually equal to the kind of loss. But when sadness is coupled with a sense of futility about the future, that is despair. When people find themselves in a state of despair, quick pastoral and lay pastoral intervention is necessary. The job of the clergy and the lay pastoral caregiver is to provide hope, to encourage, to give the parishioner a reason to go on. When someone is left alone due to the death of a spouse, they sometimes give up. A job helping in the office, or calling on the "shut ins," or folding the bulletins can give them a sense of being needed. These dynamics of grief can be found in small or large degree depending on the loss and the circumstances of it. When we think about the elderly and death, once again, they will suffer more from loss than any other age group. Helping them deal with these losses should be a priority of the church's pastoral ministry.

I have found that the major dynamic of the inner experience of grief is that of anxiety. All of the behavioral responses that we observe in grief, including fear, seem to be related to anxiety. If anxiety is the perception of a threat to ourselves, then it is easy to see how it relates to fear. Being in a situation similar to one that caused harm or discomfort earlier in our lives produces some anxiety. Just remembering the discomfort produces anxiety.

We have all experienced separation anxiety from our childhood, either when we went off to school, or summer camp, or college. We were anxious because we were not sure what the new experience would bring. We did know what we had and how to function in it. The same would be true regarding our anticipation of death. Our anxiety would be the fear of not knowing concretely what will happen after death beyond our hope of God's eternal love. Questions arise at funerals that indicate that perhaps for the first time, people are asking about life after death, the nature of God and who and what they are compared to other forms of existence. Death makes us contemplate these things, and in that contemplation, feel anxious about not only the person who died but about ourselves and what might become of us.

Elizabeth Kubler-Ross wrote *On Death and Dying* more than 30 years ago, which began a more open and frank discussion about death, preparing for death, and dealing with the death of a loved one than any work I have seen since. Dr. Elizabeth Kubler-Ross identified five stages of grief. Over the years they have become widely accepted. They are denial, anger, bargaining, depression, and acceptance. A brief review of these stages will help the lay pastoral caregiver be better prepared to minister to someone who is grieving.

Denial of the loss of a loved one is a feeling of shock and disbelief. People may tell themselves that their loved one is not dying, that there has been a mistake.

Anger surfaces in many ways, through emotional outbursts, or by placing blame on others or holding resentment toward others. Anger at God is common during this stage as are feelings that the death is undeserved or somehow unfair.

Bargaining is often referred to as a temporary truce, this stage is marked with 'If only . . ." statements. People want to make a bargain to have life return to the way it used to be.

Depression is the stage where public grieving begins. There are times of intense sadness and withdrawal. It's hard to get motivated, to get out of bed. Life seems to have lost purpose.

Acceptance is final stage and is marked with the reality of the death and the change it has created in the lives of the survivors. Finally, in this stage people are able to let go of their loved ones and continue on with live. The intense grief lessens and life takes on a new routine that lends comfort.[26]

Other reactions to grief include:

Pain: Physical pain such as an upset stomach, body aches, lack of appetite, inability to sleep

Stress: Planning funerals, paying for funerals, making decisions, interacting with families, sending thank you notes, and juggling new responsibilities all cause stress.

Anxiety: Fearfulness, a feeling that we have lost control, a realization that we, too, are mortal.

Guilt: Occasionally an accident may cause the survivor to feel guilty. Death after a prolonged illness may also produce guilt if the family member wished or prayed for an end to suffering.

Many other authors have suggested similar "stages" of death and dying. I was fortunate to hear a lecture by Dr. Alan Wolfelt, who directs the Center for Loss and Life Transition, on this topic. He identified three stages of grief. The first was what he called the "evasion of the new reality." In this stage the person goes through the normal reactions to death: shock, denial, and numbness. The normal reactions tend to help us protect ourselves against the horrible shock of accepting that one we knew and loved is dead.

The second stage Dr. Wolfelt identifies is called "encounter with new reality". Here people become anxious, panic, and are fearful because they are beginning to realize what the death will mean for their own lives. One might express explosive emotions or be irrational in blaming themselves. They may feel guilt, remorse, loss, emptiness, or sadness. One lady whose husband died got through the first stage of shock and denial, but then began to blame herself for his death because she allowed him to eat fatty foods and to sit around rather than exercise in any way. She was the classic "turtle" that blamed herself for his ill health. This is the time when questions about eternal life come up. The questions may be regarding the deceased but may also be asked as a way of reassuring oneself.

In the final stage, Dr. Wolfelt indicates that "reconciliation to the new reality" takes place. In this stage, one may feel some relief, or release; a sense of letting go. Finally there is reconciliation, acceptance. Most people get to this point. We have funeral and memorial services when a person dies as a way of helping the living. Visits to the surviving spouse or children for several months after the death of a loved one to listen to the thoughts and fears of going on alone are a good way to minister to those who have gone through the shock and anxiety associated with grief.

Reconciliation is a process that takes time. It is not an event that occurs suddenly. How long it takes for someone to move to the point of reconciliation is unique for each person. Special occasions like holidays, anniversaries, and birthdays may trigger a resurgence of feelings that the person thought they had worked through. There are, I believe, some things we must do before we can move to final reconciliation. First of all, we must accept the finality of our loss. A couple becomes a single. One's life mate is gone. They are not away on a trip, but gone. It is a hard first step. Second, our lives must begin to return to normal. Our normal sleeping and eating habits must return to what they had been. But the one we had shared our beds and our meals with will not be there. The transition is difficult. Next, we must feel a sense of release, knowing that the worst of the hurt is over and we are moving on. Some will have guilty feelings when they realize they are hurting less, as if the expectations of society were for them to morn forever. Eventually, one must begin to enjoy him/herself. Often times churches have an older adult singles group that meet for fellowship. To be finally reconciled, we must begin to live again, to move away from the grave and back into life. Perhaps the next step is most indicative of progress. We must begin to plan for the future and not continue to live in the past. Finally, we must be open to the many changes that are sure to occur.

Many people have gotten stuck at one of these points and have not become fully reconciled to the death of their spouse. One lady in a former church insisted that she be referred to as Mrs. Harold Smith* (*not her real name). She had not moved past feeling a sense of release. She certainly did not enjoy life. Most of my conversations with her dealt with her past. She seemed to have no joy. There was seldom any mention of future plans. She was stuck, and I am not sure if she has ever come to final reconciliation.

As I stated above, I believe that the second dynamic of grief is fear. I raise fear at this point to highlight something I have noticed over the years.

I believe that most of us have a fear of death. It is a fear that has its roots in the very nature of our being as a finite creature. The death of someone near to us tends to personalize death and stimulate the fear of our own impending death. This makes it difficult to discuss it or plan for it. Many people avoid preparing wills for this reason. Just talking about one's death is frightening. When someone we know dies, we begin to think about when "our time will come."

From my early childhood, I have been aware of something "spooky" about death. Ghosts, spirits, bodies rising, cemeteries, and funeral homes were all put into the category of things to fear. When someone is dead, the basic difference between life and the unknown future confronts us. As much as death is a part of life, dead bodies are not our normal experience. For that reason, we have a fear of the unknown, a fear of the dead body. Many generations ago in some parts of our country, the custom upon the death of a family member was to have the body for "viewing" in the parlor or living room of their house. People were selected to sit up with the deceased all night. I believe that part of the reason for this ritual was to ensure the safety of the family because of superstitions surrounding death, especially the fear that ghosts would visit the corpse. These superstitions go back to our prehistoric roots because of the mystery that surrounds death. There is indeed an element of fear involved in our understanding of death.

Another kind of fear we find mixed up in the emotions of death is the fear of our own suffering. Not all relationships are always smooth. If someone dies before we can share our true feelings with them, or bring about a reconciliation, we suffer anxiety and guilt for not being more kind, loving, considerate, willing to compromise, etc. Perhaps the old adage of not going to bed angry with someone has merit to it! Or better yet, perhaps we should live in such a way as not to make enemies.

My final observation about death and fear is that often times when someone dies we look at ourselves and say, "Now what am I going to do?" I have heard it many times from widows asked in many different ways.

They may feel abandoned by the spouse who has died. In past generations, often times the role of the husband and wife was clearly defined. When one died, the other was ill prepared to assume the duties once handled by the deceased. There was a clear sense, a fear, of being unable to do all that was now required.

Once again we find ourselves at the point of asking, "What can we do for those who grieve?" The image of the pastor is one that exemplifies, among other symbols, the spirit of Christ who came to comfort and to heal broken relationships. Most often, the minister can communicate God's concern. The pastor and lay pastoral caregiver can symbolize, just by their presence, that God does not forsake. Imagine how important it is to be with a family when a loved one dies. In the midst of their anger, fear and anxiety, the pastor and lay pastoral caregiver serve as symbols of hope, even without saying a word!

The role of the minister or lay pastoral caregiver in the therapy of bereavement will be proportionate to the relationship he /she had previously established prior to the death and the grief. The day I moved from my seminary apartment to my first church, I met a lady who was waiting for me on the front porch of the parsonage. Her husband had died earlier that day. How effective do you think I was at the funeral and afterwards as this lady dealt with her grief? Not knowing the person who died or the family made the funeral and comments made there seem hollow and with little impact. For this and many other reasons, it is so important to share "pastoral" responsibilities with members of the congregation. They can be an asset to the pastor as well as to the church member.

Just knowing the parishioner may not be the answer to effective pastoral care, especially if the pastor or lay pastoral caregiver is not comfortable with his/her own understanding of death and dying. Death, even for a minister, is a certain undeniable fact compelling choices of either hope or despair. The mystery, the burden of knowing one has to die, is a fact of existence. Existentialists tell us that the greatest threat experienced is the threat of "angst," the threat of non-being, hence, death. The minister's own view of death or his remembrance of poignant grief can become carried over into the relationship with the grief sufferer. This emotional baggage will color his feelings, thinking, and acting. The same can be said for the lay pastoral caregiver.

To minister to the grief sufferer, the pastor or lay pastoral caregiver must be supportive without doing the grief work for the family. They must enable the sufferer to tell of his loss, his story in his own way and in his own words. As the stories of the events prior to the death are told over and over again, it has a cathartic effect upon the teller. It becomes easier to tell and thus easier to bear. The sufferer needs those who will listen with deep and abiding concern, who will empathize with them.

Additional Resources:

Why God, by Burton Z. Cooper

When Bad Things Happen to Good People, by Harold S. Kushner

Making Sense Out of Suffering, by Peter Kreft

A Grief recovery Book: A Step-By-Step program for Moving Beyond Loss, by John W. James and Frank Cherry

Good Grief, by Granger E. Westberg

Guiding Your Child Through Grief, by James P. Emswiler and Mary Ann Emswiler

Silent Grief: Living in the Wake of Suicide, by Christopher Lukas and Henry M. Seiden

Chapter Nine Review

1. Review what Dr. Shantz says about how God suffered for humanity.
2. Think through what you believe about God causing suffering. How have you experienced suffering in life? What impact has suffering had on you?
3. Think about the power of prayer and how it can help the suffering person.

4. Practice praying for others in a variety of situations that result in suffering and sorrow, such as illness and death.

5. What are the dynamics of grief and how do you understand their impact?

6. List the five stages of death and dying identified by Elizabeth Kubler-Ross.

7. Compare the stages of death and dying proposed by Dr. Alan Wolfelt to those proposed by Dr. Kubler-Ross.

8. How do you think you would be able to support a family as a loved one dies? Where would you begin—with the Bible, with prayer, with the listening ear?

Dealing with Loss

We experience a variety of losses throughout life. At all stages of life, friends die. Life situations change because of a job loss or a divorce. Such losses affect both adults and children. Churches and communities are impacted by the loss of friends and family through death, the loss of spouse or friends because of divorce, and the loss of income and status and sense of contribution to the greater good because of unemployment. In this chapter, I am dealing primarily with the losses that affect older adults.

I was talking with a couple several years ago who were about to retire. They were excited about the prospects of travel and leisure time that lie ahead. When I visited them recently, I got a different reaction. The lady of the couple called her retirement days "a time of sorrow and pain." My reaction was disbelief. How could someone who has freedom to do what they want when they want be in pain? How could someone who now has the time to visit his or her grandchildren and travel be sorrowful? But when I listened to this couple for a while, it was easier to understand how there could be sorrow and pain.

The "happy retirement" also brought with it many losses. There was a loss of income, and so, a change in lifestyle. The husband in this couple was typical of most men in that he identified himself with his work. After retirement, these men feel a loss of identity and in some cases, a loss of worth or value. Those over age 65 suffer many losses in their later years.

It is most often during this time that one's parents die, if they have not already. As the year progress, those retirees who still have a living spouse will lose them to death. And, though it is less common, many times parents in their older years suffer the loss of their children through disease or accident. Though retirement may be a time to move to a warmer climate, such a move brings with it the loss of a house, a home, and a space that is full of memories. The loss of health is another loss commonly endured by the elderly. With the physical decline may also come mental decline. These losses, along with all those that have already been mentioned, produce stress, grief, and anxiety.

Dr. Julie Gorman teaches Christian formation and discipleship at Fuller Theological Seminary, Pasadena, California. She is a contributor to *Practical Theology for Aging*, by Derrel Watkins, and says that one common loss of this phase of a person's life as the loss of personal dignity. By this Dr. Gorman means not only things like bifocals, hearing aides, canes, and "senior moments" that all are outward signs of aging, but also the loss of remunerative work, which also leads to a loss of dignity. This is more that simply tightening the belt to match retirement income, but also a major change to the framework of the lives of the person who got up and went to work for forty-five years. It deals with socialization, responsibility, and self worth. This loss turns a world upside down. As we age we begin to depend more and more on others to provide assistance and care for us, which leads to a loss of independence. This undermines our confidence, and then we become even more dependent. Finally, we lose time. At this age, surely the future is not full of opportunities. Death is the next big passage.

All of these losses produce a feeling of unlovability—with decline in assessed worth comes a lessening of desirability and the accompanying feeling that we have less to give in loving others.[27]

When a person's health declines to the point that they must enter a Long Term Care facility, unless it is for short-term therapy, most people assume the move is the last one they will make. For many people, this is true. Perhaps that is why such moves are resisted so vigorously.

Unfortunately, most often, the elderly enter the facility directly from the hospital because it has been determined by the physician or their family that the older person can no longer live independently. They suffer many losses upon admission to such a facility, and that affects their feelings and behaviors.

The first loss, of course, is the loss of familiar surroundings. Often times the elderly have lived in their current residence for twenty years or more. Their homes are filled with furniture they have accumulated and used for forty years. Favorite pictures and easy chairs have made this place a home. Memories surround every piece of furniture, every cracked dish, every pair of slippers or sweater sent for Father's Day and Mother's Day over the years. To leave "home" is a major life adjustment. It means leaving so much of oneself, against one's will, to go to a new unfamiliar place. It means adopting oneself and one's lifestyle from living in an eight room house to only one room.

A second loss experienced when an elderly person enters a Long-Term Care facility is the loss of family contact. The family does not feel as free to drop by to visit any more. Without the extra bedrooms, it becomes expensive for the family who live out of the area to visit. As a result, they come by less often than they did before. When they do come to visit, the room is too small for everyone to sit in and there are usually only one or two extra chairs for guests. As the elderly person becomes frailer and infirmed, they may require medical attention or become confused, and the family members feel less and less comfortable coming to visit.

I have had numerous conversations with families of demented residents who speak candidly about the difficulty of a visit because their beloved relative—spouse, mother or father, uncle or aunt—no longer identifies them as a spouse or child. They are not the person they once were. Their personality has changed. Their behavior can be embarrassing. The family gets fewer rewards out of visiting and simply stops coming.

A third loss is the loss of contact with friends. Usually, by the time someone is admitted to the adult home or nursing home, they are past retirement age. The average age of those in the nursing home where I worked is 85. Most of their friends are the same age. They, too, are frail and elderly, and do not usually get out to visit. When they do, what they see in the facility reminds them that they, too, could and may soon be in a similar situation. Friends from Sunday school or the neighborhood should make an effort to visit as often as possible. They need to plan such visits; perhaps once a week or every other week at a particular time. If they are able to schedule the visit, the person in the facility can make sure he or she is available and ready for the visit.

The fourth loss experienced by every person who enters a Long-Term Care facility is the loss of control over his or her life. Life in a facility runs on the institution's schedule. Times are established to wake up, eat, take medication, participate in activities, and take a bath. The more incapacitated one becomes, the less options one is given. Doctors and nursing staff dictate what will be done when and in what manner. Food that had been prepared a certain way for forty years is now prepared by someone else who does it differently. Longstanding routines are now changed to meet the routine of the facility.

I remember explaining to a 96-year-old lady in a facility that we do not fry chicken because fried food was not good for her. She just laughed and said, "I've been eating fried food all of my 96 years. I guess it hasn't been too bad for me." She got her chicken fried that night!

Perhaps that hardest part of living in a facility is sharing a room with someone. Going from a house to a room is bad enough, but having to share that room with someone else is even harder. There is no privacy, and only room for a few personal things. The "things' that help establish our identity and remind us of our past are gone. It is indeed hard.

We had a new resident at one time who did not like the room to which she had been assigned. It was too cluttered with her roommate's wheelchair and other personal belongings. We moved her to a second room. The room was better, but the roommate played her TV and radio too loudly. Rather than ask the roommate to please turn the volume down, she asked for another room change. When we finally got to the bottom of these and numerous other complaints, it became clear that she simply did not want to be in a nursing home, and if she had to be in one, she certainly did not want a roommate. But what the residents in these facilities do not know is that Medicaid does not pay enough money for everyone to have a nice room all to themselves. The nursing home where I trained actually lost money every day on Medicaid reimbursement. It was only by virtue of the private pay residents that we could offer even a semi-private room for the poor elderly. Nonetheless, the issue for the facility operator, the social worker, and the pastor to remember is how this kind of move makes the new resident feel.

In addition to these losses, some people also suffer from physical losses that precipitate this institutionalization. Hip replacements due to severe arthritis, leg amputation due to circulation problems and diabetes, strokes, and accidents bring the elderly to a Long-Term Care Facility. Some are there for a short time, but for many, this kind of placement is most appropriate. If you couple loss of home with loss of limb, it is easy to see that the elderly in this situation need an extra amount of attention and support from their pastor and church.

The church can be very helpful in the transition from home to the Long-Term Care Facility. Pastors and lay pastoral caregivers can visit, phone, and send cards or audio and video tapes to the parishioner. These visits may go on for a few months to help the new resident get adjusted, or they may be visits that go on for many years if the church member is considered a "shut-in."

Additional Resources

Resilient Widowers: Older Men Adjusting to a New Life, by Alinde J. Moore and Dorothy C. Stratton

Transfer Trauma in Nursing Home Residents: An Annotated Bibliography, by Richard O'Hare

Handbook of Stress, Trauma and the Family, by Don Catherall

Chapter Ten Review

1. What are the four different losses that one typically goes through on entrance into a long-term care facility?
2. Compare the impact of these losses with losses experienced during other transitions
3. What can you do as a lay pastoral caregiver to assist church members who suffer loss during this difficult time?

Needs of the Elderly

Although some of the pastoral needs of the elderly are just like the needs of the younger congregation members, many other pastoral needs are unique to this group. They require the clergy and the lay pastoral caregivers to be aware of and attentive to these needs as they minister to the elderly.

When we think about the "over 65" age group, we think of a variety of needs based upon age and situation. Not every 65- year-old is in good health and not every 90-year-old is in poor health. People in the age range of 65-105 years are as vastly different, as are people from 25 to 65. Some are very active and independent while others need assistance in a variety of ways. Having said that, I would suggest that there are a few needs that most of the elderly have that the church can help meet. One of the fundamental pastoral needs of the elderly is assistance for those who suffer from both role and status attrition. It seems that the post-retirement age group faces similar problems in at least three areas.

The first common area is the loss of roles that come with retirement that excludes the aged from significant social participation and, in effect, devalues them. There are very few exceptions to the normal retirement age. Employment brings with it an identity and a sense of self-worth. As a result of retirement, the older person becomes marginal and alienated from the larger society. They tend to be tolerated, ignored, rejected, and seen as a liability. The church can find many meaningful ways to involve retired individuals in ministry. Some examples could be volunteering in the office, in the kitchen, with Meals-On-Wheels, on any variety of committees, as a usher, on the money counting team, as a mentor to young people just getting started in the business they are just leaving, and so forth. Lay pastoral caregivers need to be aware that this move from employed to retired can take its toll on people, and that often they go through a period of depression.

The second common area is that people recognize that their generation, formerly known for its contributions to society, has now moved into the new status of retirement and a set of life expectations and schedules that differ from whatever they did prior to retirement. Every phase before retirement is marked with social growth and advancement. With old age, people who were highly valued for both their performance and their achievements are suddenly redefined as old and obsolete. The real problem here is that the elderly person does not understand this new image he has acquired. For years all had gone well. He had not done anything wrong. She was not a failure. Their only crime was their age. Now the pastoral care required may simply involve helping someone adjust to being retired, helping them get involved in other kinds of activities, and expressing to these elderly that in spite of their age, they are still a person of worth.

The third area where pastoral care is necessary is in the realization that our society is not socialized to the fate of aging. During each stage of life we are prepared for the next, but not so with old age. The expectations for old age are not well defined and because there is no blue print or job description, we can hardly prepare for it. The competitive society in which we live does not prepare us to fail or lose status. The church must be prepared to assist those who find themselves in a change of role as individuals and by virtue of being "old" and to assist the elderly as they live while preparing to die. This has implications for a variety of pastoral care opportunities, beginning with the loss of a job, including in many cases the loss of a spouse, perhaps the lose of a home and with it many memories.

I am sure the church can provide pastoral care to the elderly. It has been doing it for years. In the coming generations, the church will simply have to focus more attention and energies on meeting these needs because of the growth of the aging population, the increasing life expectancy, and a shift from an understanding of church as a place to church as a community.

The area where the church is most lacking is in its understanding of how older members can be involved in ministry. We naturally think of the many ways our older members need pastoral care, but we do not often think of how they can help *provide* pastoral care. Who knows better than they who have had to adjust to loss of identity through retirement the feelings of those going through the same? It makes good sense to use the laity who have struggled through the issues we associate with aging to assist those who currently face them.

One of the mottos of the AARP is "To serve, not to be served." I believe that those who are just past retirement are able to provide any number of services for their church, including pastoral ones. They are also a good source of volunteers in other capacities. As the elderly get older, their physical abilities may prohibit them from performing the strenuous work, but they may still be of great service to others. It behooves the church to find opportunities for the older member to be in service to others. The truth is that these older adults bring wisdom, tenacity, spiritual depth, and life experiences that are valuable to our churches. They would, by virtue of experience, be good lay pastoral caregivers.

We have a unique opportunity these days to be in ministry to and with an age group (retirement age to well beyond 100 years of age) that continues to expand. Pastors and lay pastoral caregivers need to be aware of the needs of the older adults as well as their abilities as we attempt to minister to them and to assist them as they minister to others.

Mental/Psychological Needs of the Elderly

Though the other parts of our body are important for clergy and lay pastoral caregivers to understand, the brain and its potential aging difficulties will give us greater clarity in interpreting the behavior of many of our elderly church members.

Some normal changes occur in the nervous system as we age. One major misconception about the aging brain is that neurons are lost daily, and that at advanced ages there are half as many as when we were younger. A statistic frequently heard is that we lose 100,000 neurons a day. But what we do not hear is that the brain normally contains a trillion neurons. So even if we did lose 100,000 a day for each of the 365,000 days in a 100-year life span, that would still be only .5% of the total with which we started. That seems hardly significant. Successful brain aging results in some loss of complex reaction time and speed in responding to questions, but no major losses in the ability to learn, remember, or perform routine mental tasks.

Psychologists identify two kinds of intellect. The first, fluid intellect, represents limits imposed by the mechanics of the central nervous system. It is independent of the content to be learned. This kind of memory does decline with age. Crystallized intellect represents the facts, rules, and procedures we have learned over our lifetimes, especially our strategies for solving problems. Crystallized intellect involves reading, writing, and judgment. Only very late in life does the crystallized intellect decline. If we continue to challenge ourselves intellectually, it should increase over most of our lives.

When assigned to a parishioner who has mental challenges, it is important that the lay pastoral caregiver spends time getting to know as much as possible about his or her condition before the first visit. It is easy to get health information online or in a library. If the congregation has a nurse or doctor, it might be good to use them as a resource to provide basic information about mental illnesses so that the lay pastoral caregiver will feel more prepared for the assignment.

Stroke

One of the major brain related problems that seems to plague the older adult is the high risk of cerebrovascular accidents (CVA's), more commonly known as a *stroke*. The stroke is the most debilitating accidents an elderly person can face. In the United States, 400,000 people have strokes annually, with one third dying from the insult. Strokes are the third leading cause of death. Many older adults suffer from strokes that have caused memory loss or paralysis. The cause of strokes is lack of oxygen to the brain. Blood carries the oxygen, so the lack of oxygen is usually the result of blockage of a major blood vessel called thrombotic strokes; or perhaps, the leakage of blood from a vessel that has ruptured, called hemorrhagic strokes. It is estimated that 60% of the cerebral vascular accidents are due to arterial thrombosis.[28] Hypertension is a major culprit in hemorrhagic strokes. If blood clots occlude a vessel very briefly, they may cause a transient ischemic attack we call TIAs. TIAs are usually defined as temporary neurological deficits, which resolve within several hours. I will talk more about the effect of these "mini-strokes" later.

In many patients, there is partial recovery of the functions normally served by the damaged area, presumably because of transfer of these functions to other regions of the brain, which remain intact. Theocratically, this requires some reorganization of the synaptic connections within the brain. The damage to the brain affects our bodies in many ways.

Treatment of stroke involves several stages. The first involves minimizing the initial stroke damage. Recently, a clot-dissolving drug was approved for treatment of thrombotic stroke. This drug works best when administered shortly after the stroke. The second stage of stroke treatment is the recovery stage. Here, the physical, speech, and occupational therapy are extremely valuable. Encouraging the stroke patient to stick with the hard work demanded of them by the therapists is very important. There seems to be a critical time frame after a stroke when plasticity is occurring. If new functions are not regained during this time frame of a few months, the stroke victim may never recover. The third stage, often concurrent with the second, is to control the risk factors for further strokes. Reducing hypertension, correcting high cholesterol, cessation of smoking and beginning a physical exercise routine can all reduce the risk of future strokes and heart attacks. Reduction of alcohol intake and control of diabetes are also valuable. Studies have shown that aspirin has benefit in decreasing the potential for platelets to form clots. In some individuals, a surgical procedure, carotid endarterectomy, may open narrow regions of the major artery to the brain and reduce stroke risk.

Some of the common results of a stroke may be aphasia, which is the inability to interpret and understand words; dysphasia, which deals more with the inability to speak; and paralysis of one side of the body leaving the person unable to walk or use one arm.

If stroke victims are uncomfortable coming to worship, sending a cassette or videotape to their home will help them continue to feel like they are a part of the congregation. It would be even better if especially trained laity could take the materials along with a bulletin at an appointed time to share "Worship" with the stroke victim.

One of the residents of an assisted living facility I managed suffered from a stroke. Her right side was paralyzed and her speech was affected. She was a delightful lady who had been a faithful church member. Though she could not speak, she was a faithful attendee at our weekly chapel services. One day, we were singing a hymn, and this lady began to sing! We were all astonished. In this case, she could not form the words she was thinking, but could sing the old hymn that was part of her long-term memory.

Nearly every congregation includes people who have suffered from a stroke. We must be attentive to these special needs. Having handicap access enables these church members to continue to participate in worship. Someone who uses a walker may not have enough room between the pews in the sanctuary. They could sit down front, of course, but that front row seat often seems reserved for the pastor's family! The simple act of standing for hymns may be difficult for someone who uses a walker. They need the walker for support. Without it, standing may not be very easy. The pews we have in most of our congregations do not offer any arms like a chair that would to enable the older person to push him- or herself up. Perhaps it would be good to reserve the end of the pews for those who need this added assistance. Another option would be to buy stackable chairs with arms that can be placed strategically through the sanctuary for our older members, especially those who have suffered from a stroke. When we share the Eucharist, most churches invite the congregation to come to the front of the sanctuary or to a station where persons are serving the bread and cup. Someone with a walker would find this difficult and may feel like they were holding others up. In like manner, when we offer an altar call, the person who has suffered from a stroke may find it too difficult to make his or her way to the front. I encourage you to borrow a walker and try to walk through the crowd to say good morning to the pastor one Sunday. Use it during worship, and you will soon be going to the worship committee to talk with them about changes needed in the order of worship as well as sanctuary design.

Physical conditions like those that result from a stroke are easy targets for people who like to make fun of an others inability to walk or talk. It behooves the church to learn how to deal with our brothers and sisters who have suffered from a stroke, and to serve as an example of how to love those who make us feel a bit uncomfortable in their impairment.

If stroke victims are made to feel uncomfortable coming to worship due to physical conditions or attitude, they will not come back. They may choose to stay at home because it is simply easier to do so than to hassle with the many obstacles we place before them. In that case, sending a cassette or video tape of the service to them will help them still feel like a part of the congregation in some small way.

Dementia

Dementia is a term that broadly defines cognitive loss. Nearly half of all dementia are as a result of Alzheimer's Disease. Twenty percent of all dementia are due to multi infarctions, or "mini strokes." Another 15 % is a combination of Alzheimer' Disease and strokes. The remaining 15 % is made up of other diseases like Parkinson's, Huntington's, Creutzfeldt-Jakob, Picks, and depression.

It is nearly impossible to fully appreciate the plight of a demented adult. The greater the degree of brain damage in given regions, the more memory is destroyed. The following exercise may help stimulate your thinking about the needs of the demented adult.

Imagine that you wake up in the morning. You look around and you do not know where you are. Next to you in bed is someone whom you do not know. You need to use the toilet, but do not know where it is. So, you begin to roam around the house, filled with strange things, and many doors. There are too many doors, too many options. You do not find the bathroom because you are not sure if you were going out of the room or going into it, and you check the same door several times. You do not find the bathroom in time. You wet your underwear, pajamas, and footies. This is uncomfortable and embarrassing and so you take them off and begin to search around for someone or something that is familiar. Though you do not know where you are, you know where you should be; at home, the home you lived in years ago. Eventually you find the kitchen and look for some food. There is a toaster so you look for some bread. When you put the bread in the toaster, you forget about it (out of sight, out of mind) and continue to look for something else, something that may seem familiar. Finding nothing, you go out the door onto the sidewalk. Not knowing which way to go, you decide on a way and begin to walk. At the end of the block, you cross the road and nothing seems familiar. Cars go by, models you do not recognize. People go by and look and stare at you. You cannot remember where you were, but do remember where you want to go. And so you continue walking, not sure you are going the right way, but you continue to walk.

If you were in a facility like an Assisted Living Facility or a Nursing Home, the scenario would be a little different. Someone in a uniform may come into your bedroom to wake you for a bath before breakfast. You may not know them and wonder why they are in your bedroom. Where is your spouse? Someone says, "Good morning", but you don't him or her. They tell you it is time to get up and change your diaper and get a bath. You are not sure you want some strange person touching or washing you. You protest. The person talking to you seems nice enough and does seem somewhat familiar. She insists that you get undressed. You do not want to get undressed, changed, and bathed. You refuse. You tear off your diaper and get out of bed. Though unsure where you are, you are sure that you what no parts of the person in uniform giving you orders. You start to go to what must be an exit, to get away, but the lady with the clean diaper in her hand stops you and tells you to come with her toward another door. You do not know what is behind that door, but you know that you do not what to go there. You pull your hand free, hit the lady and run as fast as you can out the door from which you were just pulled away.

The days above that you were imagining oftentimes get worse than the ten minutes it took you to think through in the exercise. They may include police picking you up or medication that makes you sleepy. All of it is frightening and strange. None of it makes any sense to you. And you ask constantly for someone to give you an explanation, only to forget it and ask for it once again.

Alzheimer's Disease, the largest cause of dementia, is a progressive brain disorder affecting memory, thought, behavior, personality, and eventually, muscle control. Symptoms of include a gradual memory loss, decline in ability to perform routine tasks, disorientation in time and space, impairment of judgment, personality change, difficulty in learning, and loss of language and communication skills. The disease eventually leaves its victims unable to care for themselves.

The Alzheimer's Disease and Related Disorders Association, Inc. estimates that the disease affects as many as four million Americans. Ten percent of those adults over age 65 have the disease. Forty-eight percent of those adults over age 85 have the disease. The Association states in its statistics sheet published in 1993 that Alzheimer's Disease is the fourth leading cause of death among adults, that it primarily affects people over age 65, but can strike people in their 40s and 50s, that someone with the disease can live from three to 20 years and that the cost of home care for someone with the disease averages about $18,000 per year.

This is indeed a costly disease, monetary and emotionally. Many families try to meet the needs of their elderly parents. The typical pattern is to hire someone to act as a caregiver in the home of the parent, where the parent is are most comfortable. Often times, problems arise as the disease progresses and the need for oversight becomes a 24-hour a day job. The next step usually is moving the parent with Alzheimer's into the adult child's home. There are now many adult daycare centers available that will accommodate the Alzheimer's victim. These programs offer a degree of assurance that the adult child can continue to work because they eliminate the fear of a caregiver not coming to the house due to the caregiver's illness. As the disease progress, incontinence often becomes a problem. Difficulties arise with the parent with Alzheimer's wandering away from home. This disease often also affects ambulation. For many people, an institution such as an assisted living facility or a nursing home is the final answer. Each step along the way is more costly emotionally and financially than the one before.

Unfortunately, there is no known cure for Alzheimer's Disease. There are currently two drugs that have been approved to treat Alzheimer's: "Cognex" and "Aricept." Both these medications work by increasing the availability of a brain chemical called acetylcholine, which is involved in memory. These are treatments and not cures. They can produce improvements for a short while, and are used most often when the victim is in the early stages of the disease. The hope is that through research, a cure will be found soon so that the four million people who currently suffer from this disease will be the last.

The Alzheimer's Association issued a report of ten warning signs:

1 Memory loss
2 Difficulty performing familiar tasks
3 Problems with language
4 Disorientation to time and place
5 Poor or decreased judgment
6 Problems with abstract thinking
7 Misplacing things
8 Changes in mood or behavior
9 Changes in personality
10 Loss of initiative

I have found that it is good to know these signs because they help me better understand the world in which the Alzheimer's victim lives. The first is that those people who have dementia not only forget things, but also do so more often and do not remember them later. A second sign is difficulty performing familiar tasks. People with Alzheimer's Disease could prepare a meal and not only forget to serve a dish, but forget that they cooked it all together. Problems with language is identified as a third sign of the disease. The Alzheimer victim may forget simple words or perhaps substitute inappropriate words, making conversations vary difficult to follow. The forth sign noted is disorientation of time and place. Someone with Alzheimer's Disease may get lost in their own neighborhood and not have any idea how to get home. Though it is not restricted to demented people, poor or diminished judgment is the fifth warning sign. The victim may forget they are dressed and add another layer or a second or third hat. They may not wear anything at all. Many of us have problems balancing our checkbook, but often times the Alzheimer's victim may look at all those numbers and forget what they represent. Perhaps the thing that we think of first when we see Alzheimer's Disease is forgetfulness in that we misplace items. Often times misplaced items are found in some very unusual places. Rapid mood swings or behavior changes are also a sign of the disease. The ninth sign is similar to the previous one, but deals with personality changes. Often Alzheimer's victims become distrustful or paranoid. It is often true that folks like retired clergy end up swearing and acting ugly, which was not their nature before developing the disease. The final warning sign for Alzheimer's victims is a loss of initiative. They lack the desire to begin new projects or to do anything on their own.

Use these warning signs as a basis for planning ministry to church members who have dementia, especially of the Alzheimer's type. When the pastor becomes aware that a parishioner has this kind of a disease, they can visit and assign a lay pastoral caregiver to visit often. Depending on the extent of the dementia, the parishioner may not remember previous visits which may make this particular ministry difficult. They will remember what they learned as a child and young adult. Their faith will not be developed as one might expect, but they have the faith development of a teenager or earlier. Music, prayers, and songs learned as a child will be retained. Symbols like the cross or candles or stained glass still carry a lot of meaning for them. Communion may mean a lot even though they may not be able to participate verbally. One of the tasks for the pastor and perhaps a parish nurse is to try to educate the congregation to be accepting of these victims so that they may be able to continue to worship with the congregation.

In the early stages of the disease, Alzheimer's victims are often tearful because they realize that there is something wrong. As the disease progresses, anxiety and agitation become more prevalent. Depression is one of the next things that becomes obvious, along with purposeless activities like pacing or tapping. Suspiciousness and paranoia go along with delusions that often occur as the disease progresses. Many times there is a fear of being left alone and verbal outbursts that may make no sense. These kinds of behavior are common of people with Alzheimer's disease.

What can the church do for victims and families in the midst of this struggle? Often times, families become embarrassed by the behavior of the Alzheimer's victim. They stop coming to worship. Respite care to allow a spouse to participate in worship or other church activities may be difficult to arrange.

Multi Infarct Dementia is similar to Alzheimer's Disease in that it produces a loss of intellectual function, but the reason for that loss is different. In this case, the loss is due to multiple strokes (infarcts) in the brain. These strokes may damage areas of the brain responsible for a specific function and can also produce generalized symptoms of dementia. Someone who suffers from multi-infarct dementia may be paralyzed on one side and display loss of memory or exhibit poor judgment. Like Alzheimer's disease, multi-infarct dementia is not reversible or curable. The use of brain scanning techniques, such as CT scans and MRI's can identify strokes in the brain and further identify this particular kind of dementia. Those who suffer from multi infarct dementia have some days that are better than others regarding recall and judgment, but as the brain suffers more and more damage from these mini strokes, it will decline in much the same way an Alzheimer's patient declines. Slowly, but surely, the brain is destroyed by small blood clots. The effected area dies from lack of oxygen and glucose.

Parkinson's Disease is a progressive disorder of the central nervous system, which affects more than one million Americans. Those who have Parkinson's disease lack the substance dopamine, which helps control muscle activity. Late in the course of the disease, some Parkinson's victims develop dementia and eventually Alzheimer's disease. Conversely, some victims of Alzheimer's disease develop symptoms of Parkinson's disease.

Huntington's Disease is an inherited, degenerative brain disease, which affects the mind and the body. The disease usually does not begin until mid-life, and is characterized by intellectual decline, involuntary movements of arms, legs and facial muscles, personality changes, memory disturbance, slurred speech, impaired judgment and psychiatric problems. Huntington's disease affects more than 25,000 Americans. Although there is no treatment to stop the progression of this disease, the movement disorders and the psychiatric symptoms can be controlled by medication.

Creutzfeldt-Jakob Disease is a rare, fatal brain disorder that is caused by a transmittable infectious organism. The symptoms of Creutzfeldt-Jakob disease include failing memory changes in behavior and a lack of coordination. As the disease progresses, mental deterioration becomes pronounced, involuntary movements appear, the victim may become blind, develop weakness in the arms or legs, and in time, lapse into a coma.

Picks Disease is another rare brain disorder, which, like Alzheimer's is difficult to diagnose. Disturbance in personality, behavior, and orientation may precede, and initially be more severe, than memory defects.

Depression

Depression in the elderly is more common than many people believe. It is estimated that the lifetime risk for depressive disorder is on the order of

10-15 %. It is invoked by sadness, inactivity, loss of appetite, difficulty in thinking and concentration, feelings of hopelessness, and sometimes suicidal tendencies. Depressed persons often have some mental deficits that include poor concentration and attention. Those who suffer from depression often times experience loss of memory of "how to" perform certain functions, the ability to recognize people they have known for years, and the ability to speak.

Some degree of depression after a major loss is relatively normal. When you think about this age range (65 +) you know there must be major losses encountered during these years. Death is a constant companion. Spouses, parents, friends, and even children may die during these senior years. There is also the loss of jobs, identity, house, and positions in the community. However, if these losses cause depression that is so severe as to interfere with the activities of daily living, or extends beyond six months, the person may be a candidate for treatment.

A man and his wife made arrangements to move into the assisted living facility where I worked. Before they could move in, the man had a heart attack and went to the hospital. Upon discharge, he moved into the suite prior to his wife. She would stay at home for a few weeks and continue to prepare to make the move. A few days later, he had another heart attack and died. His wife eventually moved in as planned, but she became very depressed. Her only daughter had died six months earlier. Her husband had died. She had moved from a home she lived in for thirty-five years. She had been a golfer and enjoyed her days at "the club," but she did not drive and could not go there by herself. She also had been a smoker but was not allowed to do so in the facility. Her life was completely changed. It is no wonder that she became depressed. She had three major changes within six months and she was lost. She felt alone. She talked about suicide but was afraid that if she killed herself, she would not be reunited with her loved ones in heaven.

Day after day she talked about her plight. She cried many times a day, and told anyone who would listen about how much she missed her daughter and husband. It got to the point that other residents would ignore her because they had heard her story so many times. They, too, had issues and concerns. But, with the help of some medication, visits from her pastor, and time, she was able to become less anxious, more independent, and far less depressed. As time went by, she would tell me that she was felling a little down, but that was much improved from what she felt for several months after coming into our facility.

Dr. John Taylor, at a recent seminar I attended on depression, indicated that for those who are over age 85,:

- Men are at risk of depression 12 times greater than women.
- Protestants are more likely to commit suicide than others.
- Those who are deeply religious are less likely to commit suicide than others.
- Whites have a higher suicide rate than non-whites.
- Married people are less likely to commit suicide than those who are single.
- Those who are blue-collar employees or who have low paying jobs are at greater risk than the converse.

One of the potential problems depressed adults face is alcoholism. Those who are depressed often turn to alcohol as a means of self-medication. The stresses of aging with its losses and depression can lead to suicide or alcoholism. White males living alone and who are depressed are most likely to turn to alcohol. Those elderly who are both depressed and alcoholics are five times more likely to commit suicide.

This helpful checklist will assist in determining if a parishioner is depressed. The key is to ask if any of the following symptoms have persisted for more then two weeks. If four or more of these symptoms are present, you should refer this parishioner to a doctor.

   ____ A persistent sad, anxious, or "empty" mood.
   ____ Loss of interest or pleasure in ordinary activities, including sex.
   ____ Decreased energy, fatigue.
   ____ Unusual irritability.

___ Excessive crying.

___ Recurring aches or pains that do not respond to treatment.

___ Sleep problems, such as over sleeping.

___ Eating problems such as loss of appetite or weight loss or gain.

___ Difficulty concentrating, remembering things, or decision-making.

___ Feelings of hopelessness or pessimism.

___ Feelings or guilt or worthlessness.

___ Thoughts of death or suicide.

The depression, which occurs without a precipitating event, is called endogenous depression. In its most severe form, it is virtually incapacitating. The victim losses a desire to get out of bed, eat, put on make-up, or shave. There is no motivation to do anything. In these cases, the intervention of a physician is necessary.

Clinical depression is a whole body disorder. It can affect the way you think as well as the way you feel. For those people who are 65 or older, as many as three out of 100 suffer from clinical depression. It can be serious and in many cases, even result in suicide. The good news, however, is that nearly 80% of the people with clinical depression can be treated successfully. Even the most serious depressions can be managed with the right combinations of medication and therapy.

There are two types of clinical depression. The first is major depression. It this case, it is impossible to carry on usual activities such as sleeping, eating, or enjoying life. One is consumed by the depression and becomes more and more lethargic. This kind of depression may occur once in a lifetime, or may occur several times over. Only professional treatment can help a person with this kind of depression. A second kind of clinical depression is Bipolar Disorder. This depression leads to mood swings from extreme lows to excessive highs. These swings occur in cycles and are controlled with medication. The high part of the cycle is called mania. The low part is depression. While manic, the person seems to have boundless energy and enthusiasm. The opposite is true while depressed. This kind of depression usually starts when people are in their twenties. It requires continual treatment to keep it in check.

I had a parishioner who suffered from manic depression. She would take her medication for a while and feel fine. Then she would stop taking it because she thought she was better. The cycles of highs and lows would start all over again.

There are multiple treatments available that accelerate recovery from depression. Cognitive and behavioral psychotherapy have benefit in treating mild depression. A variety of anti-depressant medications are now available. Each has its value and some have negative side effects. As pastors, our job is not to play doctor, but to encourage our church members to visit their physicians for assistance during this difficult time.

Depression has classically been viewed as increasing with age, but some recent data indicates just the opposite. Though age does not seem to be a determining factor, sex does. Women are reported to have depression more often than men overall.

How can the church minister to people who have one or more of the diseases I have mentioned above? Our support should be for both the victim and the family.

Symbols of the church may still carry meaning to people with dementia. Music can be soothing for the demented adult. Religious songs that have been sung since childhood may be recalled in spite of some kinds of memory loss. Fellowship is important to everyone, but large crowds are difficult for the demented to handle. They may become agitated because they are not sure what to do or how to act. They are confused. Small groups and one-on-one visits are much better ways to have fellowship with the demented. Sunday School class members or choir members could provide pastoral visits to the demented adult who no longer functions well in a hall or worship setting. These adults require our help. We need to minister to them and their needs.

Home health nurses or faith community nurses can be a very practical kind of program for a church to begin. Nurses who understand dementia can be trusted to care for our elder church members. Adult daycare programs are another service churches can offer to the elderly and their families. Many churches already have childcare centers or preschool programs. Adult daycare centers are similar. In fact, they compliment each other in many ways. The older adults can volunteer in the childcare center as "baby rockers." They could spend supervised time each day in the infant room, sitting in the rocking chairs, humming or singing softly to the children that need attention and affection. For the older adult, the effect of rocking and singing was quite calming. Though many older adults who come to an adult daycare center have some physical needs, most are able to perform this task, and both they and the babies could benefit.

Their spouses and families need our assistance, physically and emotionally. Picking up a few groceries for a friend whose spouse is demented is easy for us, but greatly appreciated by the families. When I was the Executive Director of the Hampton Roads Chapter of the Alzheimer's Association, I received a phone call from a man who said, "Talk to me before I hit my Dad in the face." This caregiver was at the end of his rope. He was so frustrated because his father was irrational, never seemed to pay attention to what he was just told and insisted that he needed to go home for dinner. If we could give the spouse/caregiver a break during the day for him or her to run some errands, they will come back refreshed and better able to deal with the frustrations that come from caring for a demented adult 24 hours a day.

Spiritual Needs of the Elderly

In addition to understanding the physical and psychological make up of older adults, it is also important to understand the spiritual dimension of their lives. Dr. Harold Koenig, in his book *Aging and God*, defines spiritual needs as a "conscious or unconscious striving that arise from the influence of the human spirit on the biopsychosocial natures. They are a consequence of an inherent human impulse to relate to God, and also reflect God's influence on and desire to relate to humanity. Spiritual needs stem from a recognition that human life is finite and that there is a higher purpose to which people are called."[29] Those who are older or medically ill are confronted by the reality that they may die. Those who are healthy may be able to ignore concerns about death or life after death, but when one has been told by a physician that there is nothing more they can do, some of the 14 needs Dr. Koenig identifies come readily to the surface:

1. The need for meaning, purpose, and hope.
2. The need to transcend circumstances.
3. The need for support in dealing with loss.
4. The need for continuity.
5. The need for validation and support of religious behaviors.
6. The need to engage in religious behaviors.
7. The need for personal dignity and sense of worthiness.
8. The need for unconditional love.
9. The need to express anger and doubt.
10. The need to feel that God is on their side.
11. The need to love and serve others.
12. The need to be thankful.
13. The need to forgive and be forgiven.
14. The need to prepare for death and dying.[30]

As older people approach death either due to physical illness or simply by virtue of having lived a long life, they need some assurance that life has been for something, that life has meaning and purpose, and that their struggles have been worth the effort. Those who are religious hang on to the hope that there is more to life than the pain and suffering they may be currently experiencing. If death is eminent, the hope is for an afterlife. In some cases, illness and suffering may be seen as God testing a person, or the will of God. Depending upon what one believes, their faith may inspire them and provide them with purpose to fight on another day.

The second spiritual need, to transcend circumstances, can be seen in this example. Someone who is dying of cancer may get to the point where they are no longer concerned about themselves, but are able to get beyond their own condition to contemplate the hereafter. Their faith inspires them to move on in spite of their immediate circumstances.

The third need is for support in dealing with loss, especially death.

The elderly face death often. Besides their parents, sometimes their children die. Many times their friends die.

The fourth spiritual need Dr. Koenig identifies is the need for continuity. This is true for all people, but especially for the elderly who are suffering from some form of dementia. The structure and order helps those who are having a difficult time with memory continue to function on their own. When you think about continuity, review your own daily routine. I imagine you can recite step by step how you get up and get ready for the day. We are most comfortable when we operate out of a routine. We set the routine based on likes and dislikes and follow the routine because in doing so, we are comfortable. We follow the same route to work and stop at the same gas stations to buy our gasoline and morning cup of coffee. Lack of continuity, as in a move from home to a retirement community, can produce "transfer trauma." Transfer trauma is the physical and emotional changes that come from loss. One of the losses we face when we go to a hospital or Long Term Care community is the loss of control. One of the most reassuring things we find in our religious faith is our understanding that God will be there for us whenever needed. People from the Judeo-Christian background believe that God is the beginning and the end, the alpha and omega. This understanding helps to keep us centered in the face of distress.

The fifth spiritual need is for validation and support of religious behaviors. The older person may find activities like daily prayers, Scripture reading, or meditation helpful to them in coping with the stresses they face. By validating the use of this religious behavior, the older adult will be reaffirmed.

The sixth spiritual need is the need to engage in religious behavior. Bible study, prayer, and Scripture reading are examples of important religious behavior. Prayer buddies that phone one another and pray together are very important and are an activity that the elderly can be involved in easily. The residents in a Long Tern Care Community could be a part of this kind of activity by phone if their church had a speakerphone of some sort that would enable them to be a part of the conversation. They can be involved in Bible study by phone, tape or videotape. It is possible to have a mid day Bible study and lunch for the "over 65" group that would feed the body and the soul.

The seventh spiritual need is for personal dignity and sense of worthiness. Scared from surgery, deformed from a stroke, confused from dementia; older adults can easily lose their sense of dignity. Being dependent upon someone else to feed you and change your diaper can cause a negative affect on how you feel about yourself. Is this not a place where clergy or chaplains can talk to the older adult about grace and love?

The eighth spiritual need is for unconditional love. All people need acceptance and forgiveness. As we age we look back at our lives and begin to take stalk. We wonder how someone so sinful can be given grace and unconditional love.

The ninth spiritual need is the need to express anger and doubt. When we are afflicted by a serious illness or when our spouse dies, there is a natural tendency to blame God, or at least to ask why this happened. Many people blame God when bad things happen to them. Others blame themselves. Sometimes those people who blame God end up feeling guilty for having done so. All of us need to feel comfortable enough with our God that we can voice what is in our hearts, be that anger, sadness, or doubt. One strength of biblical faith is the emotional wisdom of the Psalms. The writers of the Psalms felt levels of comfort in expressing themselves to God in these very public acts of worship. Expressions of anger and sadness are part of this book. Within the psalms are prayers concerning aging (for example, see Psalm 71) and sadness (see Psalm 119:28-32). Psalms 9 and 10 offer insight for times when we feel close to God and times when we feel far removed from God. We often think of reading Bible passages, but now is a time to pray these passages. We address God as we read these psalms, and we let the psalms speak of our spiritual struggles to God.

The tenth spiritual need is to feel that God is on our side. After we get angry at God and doubt God's ability or existence, many times we come to the realization that God is on our side. For instance, when we are diagnosed with a terminal illness and need to get to the point of acceptance, we go through a process similar to the stages of grief. In this case we get angry, we express doubt, and finally we get to the point were we can say, "OK what is happening is not what I want, but with your help, God, I'll get through it." Often it takes a major event of some sort to get us to the point where we begin to depend upon God and know for sure that God is with us, no matter what.

The eleventh spiritual need is to love and serve others. This comes as a direct result of knowing that others love us, including our God. When we feel loved, we naturally want to express our love as well. It is an amazing thing. The more we share of ourselves, the better we feel about it. Don't we all feel good when we have done a good deed? This is especially true of the elderly. The older they get the more useless they feel. Their training and expertise is quickly outdated. They are no longer the president of this or that, but the past president. Their physical abilities decline and they no longer have the stamina they used to have.

The twelfth spiritual need is the need to be thankful. I do not believe that there is a greater need in our spiritual development than the need to feel thankful. It is easy to get down. It is easy to feel sorry for ourselves. It is easy to see the glass half empty. But moaning about our problems, dwelling on the negative and seething in anger about one thing or another never gets us out of the muck and back onto the road to acceptance of our situation.

The thirteenth spiritual need is the need to forgive and to be forgiven. I am always amazed at the people who go to their grave holding a grudge against someone else, or the families where one sibling does not speak to another, or at the number of people who have made a mistake and are too proud to go to the person they have offended to seek forgiveness. One aspect of Christian witness and discipleship is to forgive and to seek forgiveness. When grudges take root in us, we especially need to seek the compassionate love of Christ for ourselves and for those who have harmed us. We find clues for compassion in these words from Jesus spoken at the Crucifixion: "Father, forgive them; for they do not know what they are doing." (Luke 23:34) For many of us, our motives are unknown. We do not know why we act as we do. We do not understand our relationships with others, and we do not understand how we may have harmed others.

In the same way, those who have harmed us may not know the destructive nature of their deeds. Far better to seek forgiveness and to live in the present moment—as did Jesus—than to nurse a grudge or keep open a wound from the past.

The fourteenth spiritual need is the need to prepare for death and dying. The assurance we can give the older adult is that this life is not all there is. As the apostle Paul wrote of God's never ending love, "For now we see in a mirror, dimly, but then we will see face to face." (1 Corinithians 13:12) In 2 Corinthians 4:7-18, we read more about mortality and the reality of God's love made visible in Christ and made visible through our ministry. Notice these words of hope: "For this slight momentary affliction is preparing us for an eternal weight of glory beyond all measure....For we know that if the earthly tent we live in is destroyed, we have a building from God, a house not made with hands, eternal in the heavens." (2 Corinthians 4:17; 5:1) Pray with one another and live in the hope of God's eternity.

In *Practical Theology for Aging*, Dr. Martha Bergen identifies some spiritual needs of older adults. She says that the "most basic and yet cogent of spiritual needs for older adults, as with any age group, is that of a right relationship with holy God."[31] The assurance of life after death gives us hope. It helps people endure the suffering, pain and loneliness that often comes as people age.

The second spiritual need identified by Dr. Bergen is the need for a right relationship with other people. According to Dr. Bergen, "A part of spiritual wholeness and well-being demands loves, acceptance and forgiveness toward others."[32] If we love God, we are likely to love also our neighbors and want to be in a good relationship with them. This is a basic truth for Christians and it carries on from childhood through older adulthood. Love of God translates into love for and love of neighbor.

Additional Resources

New Beginnings: The Gifts of Aging (DVD), by Richard H. Gentzler, Jr. (Discipleship Resources, 2006)

The Healing Journey through Retirement, by Phil Rich, Dorothy Madway Sampson and ale S. Fetherling

Seasons of Goodbye; Working our Way through Loss, by Chris Ann Waters

Stroke Free for Life: the Complete Guide to Stroke Prevention and Treatment, by David Wiebers

Talking to Alzheimer's: Simple Ways to Connect When You Visit With Family a Member or Friend, by Claudia J. Strauss

Overcoming Depression: A Step-by-Step Approach to Gaining Control Over Depression, by Paul Gilbert

The Spiritual needs of Children: A Guide for Nurses, Parents and Teachers, by Judith Allen Shelly

The Lay Pastoral Worker's Hospital Handbook: Tending the Spiritual Needs of Patients, by Neville A. Kirkwood

Recognizing Spiritual Needs in People Who Are Dying, by Rachel Stanworth

Medicine, Religion and Faith: Where Science and Spirituality Meet, by Harold Koenig

Chapter Eleven Review

1. What are the common areas of concern faced by the elderly?
2. What could a lay pastor do to assist a person who is going through a difficult time adjusting to retirement?
3. How might an older adult serve as a good lay pastoral caregiver?
4. If you have opportunity to watch the dvd *New Beginnings* in a group, discuss possibilities for creative ministries with those who are aging.
5. Identify two different kinds of strokes.
6. What are the various kinds of dementia and how do these affect the elderly?
7. How can you, as a lay pastoral caregiver, minister to the person

with dementia as well as the family members?

8. Define depression and how it affects the person who is depressed.

9. Name and describe the fourteen spiritual needs Dr. Koenig identifies.

10. How do you relate to the four spiritual needs identified by Dr Bergen?

11. Imagine how you or the church may help the elderly meet their spiritual needs. What will you be able to do as a lay pastoral caregiver to help meet these needs?

The Dying Process

When diagnosed with a terminal illness, people's lives change dramatically. The feelings that surface can be overwhelming. Initially, they may include anger and fear. If they have never experienced a significant loss before, these feelings may be overwhelming.

In addition to these feelings, people who are diagnosed with a life-threatening illness may also experience physical changes. They may not sleep well, lose their appetite, treat loved ones unkindly, or strike out at those who are near to them.

The blessing of a life-threatening diagnoses is that it provides the person and the family with time to prepare for death. During this preparation time they can address personal issues and make important end-of-life decisions. This time might be used to get legal affairs in order, to prepare a will if one has not been prepared, to plan a funeral, or to say goodbye to family in a particular way that is meaningful to the person dying.

As might be imagined, the first reaction to hearing that one has a terminal illness is an emotional one. Sadness, anger, and outrage are common. It is difficult to remain calm knowing that something terrible has happened to us and that we cannot change it. Eventually, we will die.

One of the emotions we experience is grief. Grief is different for everyone and goes through a process from denial to anger to guilt to fear and confusion. The person will be upset at not being able to fulfill hopes or dreams, at not being able to see grandchildren, at not being able to travel, at holding back others who need to spend time helping them, and the list goes on.

Depression is common as people go through the stages after hearing they have a terminal illness. They may feel sad or full of despair. When depression is coupled with medications and an illness, they all serve to knock the person down.

Anxiety is also common for people diagnosed with a terminal illness. There are many unanswered questions. Terminal does not often come with a date and time. There is fear and concern that produce anxiety.

Physical decline occurs as people slowly lose abilities. It gets to the point in most diseases that people are no longer able to bathe or dress themselves, or go to the bathroom unassisted. There is often pain associated with the illness. This pain prevents people from fully enjoying what little time they do have left. They are forced to make adjustments to their normal routine, to live a different lifestyle. Breathing may be affected by the disease and oxygen may be required. It may be that digestion is affected due to the inability to eat or problems within the digestive system. There could be any number of reasons why people feel physical discomfort. The important thing to remember is that the person who is ill may not feel much like a visit some days, so it is important to honor that.

When the ill person is nearing death, it is common to see things like loss of appetite, sleepiness, confusion, skin discoloration, and uneasy breathing.

A lay pastoral caregiver's ministry to every dying person will be different, as every situation is different. The parishioner's beliefs, the attitudes of the family, their religious customs, and the convictions of the lay pastoral caregiver all influence what should be said and done.

According to Carl J. Scherzer in his book *Ministering to the Dying*, "Ministering to the dying is the most challenging of all pastoral functions, for the clergyman will need to be spiritually and emotionally sensitive to the needs of the individual and the members of the loved one's family. To be helpful, he must communicate understanding, love and faith with a great deal of the guidance of the Holy Spirit."[33] It is very important for the lay pastoral caregiver to be present, to listen, to offer support, and to let the family and the one who is ill talk or simply remain silent.

Although every situation is different, Scherzer does offer some advice that could help a lay pastoral caregiver in most situations. Most people crave security and love. In the dying process, it is important that the dying person and the family understand and accept that God loves them, and that even in death, God will care for them. This belief enables families and the dying person to accept the death and move into the final days with less anxiety. If the dying person believes that his or her family will be united again in eternal life, it also makes for an easier transition emotionally.[34]

As people near the end of their lives, emotions of guilt or fear may be displayed. They may need to talk to someone about either of these and the lay pastoral caregiver may be just the right person. Expressing guilt over a past deed may help the person feel better. If this occurs, it is best to lead the parishioner in a prayer following his or her confession asking God to forgive, and reassure the person that God is a loving and forgiving God. Expressing fear about dying is normal and is something that the lay pastoral caregiver should expect. No matter how faithful one is, there is always going to be some question about eternal life. It makes sense to be fearful. If the parishioner expresses fear, the lay pastoral giver should not condemn, but listen and reassure based on his or her own beliefs.

Additional Resources

Final Gifts: Understanding the Special Awareness, Needs and Communications of the Dying, by Maggie Callanan and Patricia Kelley

Questions and Answers on Death and Dying, by Elisabeth Kubler-Ross

Grief, Dying and Death: Clinical Interventions for Caregivers, by Therese A. Rando

A Kids Book About Death and Dying, by Eric Rofes

Chapter Twelve Review

1. Identify the typical physical response to learning that one is dying.
2. Identify some of the emotional responses to learning that one is dying.
3. Imagine how you might feel if you were diagnosed with a terminal illness or what you might do upon hearing this news.
4. If you have lost a close relative to a prolonged illness, what feelings do you recall having at that time?
5. What do you think about Rev. Scherzer's quote regarding security?

ENDNOTES

1. Erik Erikson, *Identity Youth and Crises*, (New York: W.W. Norton & Company, Inc., 1968) 91,141.

2. Gail Sheehy, *Passages*, (New York: Bantam Books,1976) 17.

3. Ibid. 29

4. Ibid. 29

5. Ibid. 30

6. Ibid. 31

7. Ibid. 46

8. Gail Sheehy, *New Passages*, (New York: Random House, 1995) 4

9. James Fowler, *Stages of Faith: The Psychology of Human Development and the Quest for Meaning* (San Francisco: Harpercollins, College Division, 1981) 182-200.

10. Rita B. Hays, *The Children's Minister* (Nashville: Discipleship Resources, 2007) 10.

11. Ibid. 11

12. Joy T. Melton, *Safe Sanctuaries: Reducing the Risk of Child Abuse in the Church* (Nashville: Discipleship Resources, 2000) 7-30

13. Ibid. pp. 13-103

14. Eugene Kennedy, *Crisis Counseling* (New York: The Continuum Publishing Corporation, 1981) 5.

15. Ibid. 5

16. Ibid. 6

17. Ibid. 6.

18. Gerald Caplan. *Principles of Preventive Psychiatry*, (New York: Basic Books, Inc. 1964) 26-55

19. Ibid. 16

20. Alexander Leaf, "Getting Old," *Scientific American* (1973), 44-53.

21. Robert L. Kane, Joseph G. Ouslander and Itmar B. Abrass, *Essentials of Clinical Geriatrics*, 2nd edition (New York: McGraw-Hill Professional, 1989) 10.

22. Malcom McConnell, "Faith Can Help You Heal," *Reader's Digest* (October 1998) 109.

23. Derrell Watkins, *Practical Theology for Aging* (Binghamton, NY: The Hawthorn Press, 2003) 59.

24. Ibid. 59

25. Kenneth Mitchell and Herbert Anderson, *All Our Losses, All Our Griefs* (Philadelphia: Westminster Press, 1983).36-46.

26. Elizabeth Kubler–Ross, *On Death and Dying* (New York: Macmillan Company, 1970).

27. Watkins, 92

28. Nancy R. Hooyman and Wendy Lustbader, *Taking Care of Your Aging Family Members* (New York: The Free Press, 1986) 140.

29. Harold Koenig, *Aging and God* (New York: The Hawthorn Press, 1994) 283.

30. Ibid. pp. 284-294.

31. Watkins, 131

32. Ibid. 132

33. Carl J. Scherzer, *Ministering to the Dying*, (Philadelphia, Fortress Press, 1963). 45

34. Ibid. 46